Rising
Above
Mediocrity

MW01298088

Roy Dobbs
Five-Term Mayor of Berry, AL

Dedication

I dedicate this book to my wife, Phyllis, who for more than 40 years has been an inspiration to me and encouraged me to continue working, remain focused, and complete this book. She has truly been the wind beneath my wings. I also thank my three children, Virginia, David and Joe, who have truly been an inspiration in my life. I thank you all for your love, dedication and encouragement.

Contents

A Blessed Journey

The journey upon which you are about to embark is based on an actual account of the life of an ordinary person who realized early in life that despite numerous obstacles he could rise above mediocrity. That realization did not come in one startling flash of lightning, but was realized over several years through many life experiences and with the help of other people.

The early years were ordinary. However, as time passed my life was filled with highs and lows, and with many ordinary, and later on a few monumental, accomplishments. Throughout the journey all the events were rewarding in that they helped me build character and a keen determination to reach the next level. It was clear early on that an average performance was easily attainable. Setting and attaining objectives beyond one's comfort zone was far more difficult, but also far more rewarding.

As I have lived in excess of three quarters of a century, in two different centuries, and two different millennia, I have been given many opportunities to reach for the gold. I didn't always attempt to excel, and on numerous occasions I was more comfortable in the pursuit of a mediocre performance. In the second 40 years of my life, I have found the added joy of doing my best, performing above my comfort zone, and setting lofty goals not easily attained. I have expected more of myself, and given more effort, and ultimately the rewards have been extremely satisfying.

God has blessed me. He has always opened my eyes and illuminated my pathway, but I now realize what the term "making a difference" really means. I truly believe the accounts described in this book can encourage and motivate others. I pose this question to anyone reading this book: Are you performing at the pinnacle of your ability, or are you content to settle for mediocrity?

My hope is that you will reevaluate your life, your ambitions, and your self-esteem and set new, loftier goals for yourself. Turn your life into a real channel of blessing for everyone around you, but most of all for yourself.

When we reach the point where we can say that all things are possible if we believe and work each and every day to make those dreams come true, only then can we expect to reach our full potential.

At first glance, you will think this book is about me and what I have accomplished in life, and you would be correct to a large degree. But it is about far more than a person; it is about life and the obstacles and opportunities life presents to each of us.

Don't think for a minute that I feel I have led a charmed life. There were plenty of disappointments and failures along the way, but I learned something from each one of them that somehow helped me get over the next hurdle. In the end, I feel the successes far outweighed the failures, and that is the lesson I hope to convey in writing this book.

Life is filled with ups and downs, failures and successes. Success is measured in many ways, but I feel the most important reward is what one feels inside by knowing that he or she did his or her very best each and every day, never settling for doing just enough to get by.

Some wise person once said that if you build a fence low enough anything or anybody can jump over it. Likewise, if you set your personal goals low enough they are easily attainable. But if you set higher goals and work hard, work smart, and persevere you can reach that higher plateau. The rewards at the top are much more gratifying.

My sincere wish is that each person who reads this book will realize that we all have a purpose in life. We may not always realize what that specific purpose is, but with God's help, a great deal of perseverance, and a tenacious attitude, no matter what troubles one faces, he or she should keep a sharp eye on the goal and never settle for mediocrity. I believe success is measured in the amount of good one does rather than in the amount of money one accumulates. I believe that deep down we all have an innate ability and responsibility to perform at the highest level possible and to do what we can to help our fellow man.

I challenge each and every reader to not squander any of the precious time you have, because all our lives are measured in the proverbial hourglass. The sands of time drift away, and we are limited in the amount of time we have to perform our tasks on this earth. I have been blessed to know many wonderful people in my life, many of whom have helped me in some way. I hope that by sharing my own experiences, accomplishments and failures that I can inspire or help others, and that by doing so I will have fulfilled my destiny.

My goal is not to lecture or boast. It is to encourage others to act, and perhaps avoid a few of the mistakes I have made, and hopefully offer a shortcut to success. It is to offer examples of ways to improve, build confidence, and grow as a person.

There is a difference between arrogance and confidence, or arrogance and courage. It takes courage to try new ideas and to risk failure. Valuable lessons can be learned from failure; it prepares you for the next attempt. Succeeding at difficult tasks builds confidence, and it takes courage to face difficult tasks. I believe that true success is achieved in one's chosen field only through courage and action, and my mission is to demonstrate that theory.

There are many simple formulas for success, but they all require action. Other buzzwords in the usual success formulas include teamwork, study, pride, loyalty, dedication, discipline, determination, leadership, charity and hard work. To that list I'd like to add courage, or the willingness to step up to a challenge. These qualities can be developed, of course; we hear and read about them from athletic coaches almost daily, and the same principles apply in every aspect of life.

I hope to awaken your senses to the opportunities and challenges we all face each day and to encourage you to perform at your highest possible level in achieving your goals in your chosen field. In doing that, you will surely rise above mediocrity, and you might well surprise yourself in the process. At each step along the way, your confidence will grow along with your skills.

Above all else, trust in God to guide your efforts. That is exactly what I did.

Early Arrival into Life

My life began on the bitterly cold morning of January 18, 1933, in the little northwest Alabama town of Berry. My mother, Gwendolyn Hall Dobbs, had experienced a difficult pregnancy with me and even had a miscarriage before conceiving me. In an attempt to extend her pregnancy with me to full term, she had taken some strong medication. In spite of all those efforts to hold me back, it was to no avail that I was destined to be a premature baby.

My early arrival was something of a surprise, and Dr. J. D. Scrivner was busy elsewhere, so my dad drove out in the country to get him while a nurse and my mother's cousin who served as a midwife stayed to help her with the early stages of delivery. According to Mother, Dad arrived with Dr. Scrivner just minutes before I arrived and all was well in the end.

My initial appearance was less than spectacular, I was later told. I was blue, wrinkled, and my breathing was shallow. I was referred to as a "blue baby." The nurse had a tub of warm water nearby, and after I was placed in the comforting warm water my appearance quickly improved. I was fortunate to survive because under the primitive conditions of that time many premature babies didn't make it. By God's grace, I did.

When I was old enough to go outside the house on my own, a brand-new world welcomed me. I discovered a vast area of territory to explore. I remember I was about four years old at that time. One day I found myself on my hands and knees peering under our house. The house was a frame home built several inches above ground level. I surveyed the open space and was tempted to explore whatever worlds might be mysteriously hidden in that dimly lit crawl space. As I inched my way under the house I encountered spider webs and a great deal of loose dirt that quickly covered my face and body.

My mother was busy working in the home at the time and soon realized that I had escaped the confines of our home, and God knows where I had wandered. She immediately dashed out the rear door of our house on Dobbs Street and began circling the house frantically, calling my name. "Roy Hall," she said, calling me by my full given name as she always did. "Roy Hall, where are you?" After a brief excursion under the house, I began to get a little frightened and crawled toward the light. As I emerged from the catacombs of the dirt, I truly was a dirty little boy in many ways for slipping out of the house knowing my mother was worried sick. As my mother picked me up and cradled me in her arms, I could feel the alarm and deep concern she had experienced. As young as I was then, I realized just how much my mother cared for me.

As I experienced the coming years with much anxiety, I always knew one fact: My mother would always be there for me, and she was until the day she passed. She was my rock and my mentor. She was 87 years old when she finally gave in to a serious stroke. My mother was more than a mother; she was my friend, but most of all she was my dear, sweet mother. She renewed my spirit when calamities arose; she shared the joy when successes came; she taught me to learn from my failures by picking myself up, dusting myself off, and moving on. Her philosophy was to never look back. "We can't do anything about yesterday; today and tomorrow is what really counts," she would say.

I remember when I was a young lad I would wish for things. I'm confident that everyone has been guilty of the same. We could say that we were almost wishing our lives away. I remember wishing that I were six years old so I could have a real birthday party. I wished I were seven years old so I could enter the first grade in school, which finally came in 1938. Five days a week in school finally became a lifetime, and I would wish for the weekend so I could visit my friends and we could ride horses and swim in Cedar Creek. I wished for the end of the school year. Yes, we wished for all those things that pleased us. I found myself wishing for my days in high school to somehow come to a successful completion. Most of us go through life wishing for events to begin then later hoping that they will soon end. We failed to realize at the time that those days and years were all very special. They were our formative years, truly the days of our lives. Each day is a special day, each year a special year—a time to seek that to which God would have us aspire.

My Mother and Father

My mother was the true inspiration and motivation in my life. She was born January 22, 1910, to Virgil Gaston Hall and Mary Johns Hall of Berry, Alabama. One of four girls, Mother was an inquisitive, adventurous young girl. She had red hair and freckles. Need I say more? Her actions were always obvious, even as a child. She said whatever she thought and willingly accepted the consequences.

Mothers are special. I certainly feel that way about mine, and I wish she were here today. My mother passed away several years ago, but her memory lingers on. She gave me life, nurtured me during my infancy, and perpetually prepared me for the awesome responsibilities of the future. She knew there would be difficult days ahead as well as pleasant ones. She provided so much tender love and care that I was always comfortable in her presence.

My mother had a deep, abiding faith in God, and she had faith in me. Her faith and strength was shared with me, and I thank God for my sweet mother. My dreams and expectations have been realized, and I truly have greater joy and contentment than I have ever known.

My father was Roy Edwin Dobbs. He was born December 15, 1909, in Berry, to Samuel Lee Roy Dobbs and Lula Dobbs. There were four boys and one girl in his family. My dad, according to my mother, was a pretty good baseball pitcher and could have been a really good athlete in high school, but he never had the necessary guidance or discipline from his parents.

My father was exposed to moonshine whiskey at the early age of 12. His maternal grandmother lived with his family in Berry, and according to my dad, his granny kept a jug of moonshine stashed in the closet at all times. Dad and his three brothers all developed an early fancy for that jug, and as a result my father wrestled with alcohol addiction most of his life. This created much discord in our family.

My mother and dad attended school in Berry. Mother was an above-average student, while dad was not interested in school work. His primary interests involved drinking whiskey and having a good time. Mother was attracted to my dad while they were in high school. My dad played football and baseball where he excelled as a pitcher. Mother said that his temper often got the best of him.

My mother was a cheerleader, and I suppose that was one reason she took a fancy to my dad. My mother reminded me that she was affectionately called "Red" because the color of her hair was blazing red. She noticed my dad had the initials "RED" on his baseball cap. Mother was sure that was to attract her attention, which it did. However, the "RED" on dad's hat was not for mother but for his name, Roy Edwin Dobbs. No matter, Mother stayed on course and declared this young man hers.

My father's drinking wasn't the only problem in this relationship. My grandfather and grandmother Dobbs were devout Church of Christ followers, although my dad and his brothers were not so faithful. They preferred to drink and carouse on Saturday night and sleep in on Sunday. My mother was a Baptist, like the rest of her family, and the difference in religious backgrounds often caused problems for our family, too.

My mother graduated from Berry High School in 1927 and entered Howard College (now Samford University) in Birmingham, Alabama. She attended Howard for only part of a year before entering nursing training at the Tennessee Coal and Iron Hospital in Birmingham, and she soon met a handsome young man named Jack Mitchell. Jack had a good job with Southern Bell Telephone Company, and he and my mother quickly became romantically involved. My dad really never seriously pursued my mother, but when he learned of her new suitor he snatched Mother away, and they eloped to Jasper and got married. I really believe that through the years Mother reflected often on her snap decision to hastily marry Dad and not Jack, and she actually said as such to me after my dad passed away.

My parents were married in 1930. I was born three years later in 1933, and my brother Joe was born November 10, 1935.

My dad was an absentee husband and father most of the time, particularly in my early childhood. He was not good at holding a regular job, and he moved away and left my mother, my brother Joe, and me to fend for ourselves on several occasions. I honestly feel he was avoiding his responsibilities as a father and provider. My mother was always there to ensure that my brother Joe and I had the necessities of life, the most important of which were love and encouragement.

Dad was a mild-mannered person until he got drunk, but he was drunk most of the time. His addiction to alcohol created monumental problems in our home and in all of our lives. I never understood the verbal abuse my dad cast upon my mother. I often wondered why he didn't just divorce her if he hated her so much. I always felt it might have been because of the Dobbs theory on religion. In those days, my grandparents on my father's side regularly expressed concern for my mother's spiritual well-being. They held to the premise that she must be baptized into the Church of Christ before she could go to heaven. My mother never considered that and held firmly to her dependence on the Lord and stayed in the Baptist Church.

For some unknown reason, my father left my mother alone in Berry with two small children and moved to Birmingham. We were not totally alone, of course, because my grandfather and grandmother Hall were always there for us.

One of my early recollections of my dad was around 1939. Dad would come back periodically to visit with us in Berry. He seemed more like a relative than a caring father. It seemed he wanted his freedom, yet he would appear now and then unexpectedly.

The train from Birmingham would steam around the bend into Berry and come to a stop at the downtown depot with the steam puffing out the side of the old steam engine. The evening mail and freight would be offloaded along with the passengers. Every so often, my dad would be one of the passengers when he occasionally made a weekend visit. As a youngster, I never really understood just why he worked in Birmingham, which required him to be away from home most of the time while my brother, my mother, and I lived in Berry.

Almost every time, Dad would be rather intoxicated upon his arrival in Berry. The policeman—we only had one—would greet the train and escort my dad directly to the little jail, where he would be charged with public intoxication. Sometimes he would not be fully drunk, so he would be spared the home away from home, one of the jail cells at City Hall. Regardless, he would seek me out, and I was always gullible enough to follow him anywhere. My mother would allow me to go with him because she expected him to visit his parents, my Dobbs grandparents.

I remember one evening Dad picked me up and we drove to Uncle Blenna Hall's house. Dad was seeking some moonshine whiskey, and Uncle Blenna Hall was known to produce some quality moonshine. The reason my dad was in search of moonshine was quite simple: The sale of beer and whiskey was not legal in Fayette County; moonshine was the only option. Uncle Blenna was a younger brother of my grandfather Hall, and since my mother always referred to him as Uncle Blenna, so did I. Dad and I approached the front porch of Uncle Blenna's rustic, wood-frame house to find him perched on the front porch dressed in his bib overalls with no shirt and no shoes. The cane-backed chair he was sitting on was propped up against one of the posts that supported the front porch.

As we approached, Dad said, "Do you have any whiskey, Blinner?" His name was Blenna; however, everyone called him "Blinner." The response was, "Sure I do, Bob;

do you have any money?" Dad responded that he did. Uncle Blenna never moved from his reclined position in that chair until after Dad produced the cash. Uncle Blenna informed Dad where to find a Mason jar of moonshine whiskey, which was strategically hidden nearby. Uncle Blenna said, "Bob, they ain't no reason for you to look, for they ain't no more in that area."

That was one of the more exciting outings my dad took me on, although he did take me fishing and hunting once or twice. He would spend a couple of days in Berry, then board the train and return to Birmingham. I never really understood why we were left behind. I wondered if we had done something wrong. I loved my Dad, and I always hoped he loved me. I never understood just what he did in the big city. Mother later explained that he was working in Birmingham because there was no suitable employment in Berry. I suppose that was a rational explanation, but it remained confusing to me why we weren't there with him.

My father was given the opportunity of working in my grandfather's store before it burned, but his drinking prevented that. I think my Dad resented my grandfather Hall primarily because of all his success. Despite the troubles in our family, my mother was always a rock.

Parents' 50th Wedding Anniversary
(Gwen, Joyce, Bob, Joe, Roy, Phyllis)

Dobbs Ancestors

We don't always understand God's goodness in providing unique experiences for each of us and allowing a diverse group of people to flow in and out of our lives. My dad's parents were different in many ways from my mother's but they were good for me, providing a balance for me and a better understanding of people and personalities that has served me a lifetime. Although they weren't outwardly affectionate, somehow I knew that they loved me and I felt secure in their presence.

My dad's father was born in the community of Sterling in Tuscaloosa County on August 30, 1878. Shortly after his 21st birthday, in the closing months of the 19th century, he accepted a job at Shepherd's Mercantile Store in Berry and subsequently moved to Berry. Like many young men of the day, he found lodging in one of the local homes that had been converted into a boarding house. It was very likely that the lady who owned the home needed money after her husband passed away and her children had moved away. The vacant rooms and her ability to cook were the primary assets that proved to be a lifesaver for her and created a reasonably profitable business, given the steady flow of young men who needed a place to live and who thrived on the enormous meals she provided.

Because the primary method of communication with folks back home was through the mail, "Big Sam" as his many close friends called him, visited the local post office every day and sometimes twice a day. It is no wonder that his desire to hear an encouraging word from home set him on a collision course directly in the path of Louella Bagwell, one of Berry's most beautiful young ladies. He decided right then and there at their first meeting that she was the girl he would marry. Although he didn't like to show his feelings, his matter-of-fact pursuit of her worked well, and he married his beloved "Ella" just six days before Christmas in 1900.

Sam and Ella set up housekeeping in a large, two-story home in north Berry where they raised four sons and a daughter: Howard William, Lurleen, Archie Leland, my father Roy Edwin, and Paul Conrad. We grandchildren lovingly referred to them as Big Daddy and Little Mama because of their contrasting physical attributes. Big Daddy was a giant of a man weighing in at more than 350 pounds, while Little Mama was a thin, petite woman.

I can still see Big Daddy in my mind today, impeccably dressed in a three-piece suit accented with a brightly colored tie carefully puffed out displaying contrasting colors, and proudly wearing a very large gold stickpin made from a $2.50 gold piece he once found on the street between Shepherd's Mercantile and the Bank of Berry. I still have that stickpin and any time I want a memory boost I pull it out and proudly pin it to my lapel.

Most homes in Berry had very little grass in their yards by choice. Residents would sweep their yards clean, removing every blade of grass. Big Daddy's yard was an exception, with a lot of grass in the yard contrasting with most of the homes around them. It proved to be the ideal place for a group of boys to engage in a challenging game of touch football. My cousins Edwin Holder and Paul "Skeeter" Dobbs lived in Birmingham but visited Big Daddy and Little Mama often. Edwin and I were the official captains of our teams. We filled the rosters of the two teams through a front-yard draft system, each choosing the best players available from the group of kids who found their way to the yard. We seldom had a real football to play with, but that didn't matter; we just stuffed one of Big Daddy's huge socks with old rags and made one.

When the fun of football subsided or the score became too lopsided, the teams disbanded and we lit out for the woods where we used up our remaining energy playing hide-and-seek, roaming through graveyards, climbing trees, running, slaying dragons, killing Yankees, and generally exploring. Mark Twain would have been proud of our group and maybe even could have learned a trick or two from this band of rapscallions.

Our adventures served us well because at the end of the day we had all worked up a huge appetite for Little Mama's cooking. Samuel Dobbs probably might have been just "Grandpa" or "Gramps" if Little Mama had not been such a good cook. Instead, he became Big Daddy from feasting on Little Mama's delicious southern meals made from such fresh vegetables as fried okra, creamed corn, peas and butterbeans served with fresh onions, hot peppers, and cornbread baked in a cast-iron skillet. Add to that fresh milk or even better, freshly churned buttermilk, and it was a meal to remember. The only time it got better was after the first really cold snap of winter when the men slaughtered hogs and fresh pork was added to the feast.

My brother Joe and I spent many nights with Sam and Ella. On cold nights, Big Daddy would drag his favorite rocking chair over near the fireplace and lift each of us onto one of his knees. He held us gently while he rocked back and forth in front of the roaring fire, squeezing us tighter and tighter as he progressed through one of his scary stories of rawhide and bloody bones, each word building on the fear of the previous word. "Bloody bones, bloody bones, bloody bones coming after young boys," he would slowly say as he allowed his upper dentures to drop down and make eerie sounds as he pushed them menacingly between his lips.

By the end of each story he had frightened the dickens out of both of us and had Joe begging Big Daddy to take him home. "If you don't want to stay Joe, the road's open, go ahead and strike out for home," Big Daddy would say with a laugh, knowing that with no street lights and facing 20 minutes alone in the dark to walk home us boys could not muster the courage to accept his dare.

He knew we were more afraid of what might be waiting in the darkness to rip our tender flesh right off our bones than the stories he told. Although we were frightened, we felt safe with our grandparents and always chose to stay in Big Daddy's protection rather than risk what may be lurking outside.

Dobbs Grandparents
(Ella and Sam)
(Little Mama and Big Daddy)

Daddy Hall

My grandfather, Virgil Gaston Hall, was my early role model. He was a merchant and farmer, and his sharecroppers called him Mr. Hall or "Boss." His close friends called him Virg. His daughters very respectfully referred to him simply as Papa. We grandchildren affectionately called him Daddy Hall.

Daddy Hall was a tall, thin man with a level disposition and a solid business head. Born on April 17, 1885, Daddy Hall had only a third-grade education, but he quickly realized that hard work would be required to make his youthful dreams of success become reality. He married Mary Johns, a schoolteacher, on December 23, 1906, and together they successfully pursued their dreams. They opened a mercantile store in Berry in the early 1900s as co-owners with Sam South, a cousin of Daddy Hall's. Later my grandfather bought Mr. South's interest, it became V. G. Hall, and Company and my mother became a one-fourth partner in that business.

We referred to Grandmother Hall as Mama Hall. She was a great cook and a wonderful, compassionate lady. We loved her very much. My earliest recollection of Christmas is with all our family gathered in the big living room of Grandmother and Grandfather Hall's home in downtown Berry.

As a young lad, Christmas was always filled with excitement and expectations for me. Daddy Hall had an employee by the name of Cannell. At least that's all I ever knew him by. In 1939, Christmas came and a large Christmas tree was set up in the front room of my grandparents' home. Santa Claus came into the room with a big red suit and impressive white beard. I snuggled close to my mother, not sure just what was happening. My birthday was in late January, and I had not yet entered first grade. I think I still believed in Santa, or at least wanted to. Santa opened the door to the bedroom and rolled in a sidewalk bicycle—my first bike. I had never ridden a two-wheeler, therefore, there were some bumps and scrapes but I soon conquered the task of balance and forward motion. Daddy Hall gave each of his four daughters a new Chevrolet sedan for Christmas that year, too.

Daddy Hall and I had many memorable moments and adventures together. I recall vividly that one day he instructed me and my cousin Paul to chop and clean the onion bed in the garden. He always planted a large garden for the entire family. Now, when one said chop and clean that generally meant to take a hoe and rake and cut all weeds and the like that appeared above ground. We did just that until the onion bed was clean. When Daddy Hall came to check our work he was dismayed. He said, "Why did you cut all the onion tops off?" My response was simple. "You said clean the bed." He was surely upset with us, but he just calmly pointed out what we should have done and left it at that, teaching us more than one valuable lesson with his kindness.

On one occasion, I was invited to accompany my grandfather on a vacation to Hot Springs, Arkansas, and then on to Texas. A couple of days before departing he instructed me to go to the Bank of Berry and get some cash for our trip. My grandfather was the co-founder and vice president of the bank. I proceeded to the bank, and as instructed I approached the counter and saw Phelan Shepherd, bank president and co-owner. Mr. Shepherd said, "Roy Hall, what can I do for you today?" I explained that Daddy Hall had instructed me to get $100 for our upcoming vacation to Hot Springs, Arkansas. He counted out the cash, handed it to me without any paperwork, and I went back to the store and gave the money to my grandfather. After receiving the $100 and thinking about it for a few minutes, Daddy Hall said he thought we might need a little more money and sent me back to get another $100.

Our trip to Arkansas then on to Texas was filled with adventure. My grandfather and I had many wonderful times together, and I count myself fortunate to have had such a caring grandfather as a friend. I recall receiving a letter from him in the summer of 1947. We were living in Birmingham, and he was living in Berry. In the letter, he invited me to accompany him to Hot Springs, Arkansas, where he thoroughly enjoyed the hot mineral baths. He said it made a new man out of him.

Well, he had a new Frazer automobile. If one can remember that right after World War II, automobiles were not yet in full production and Mr. Henry J. Kaiser had been in shipbuilding during World War II. He apparently had lots of leftover parts, so he decided to use them to construct automobiles. My grandfather had the top-of-the-line Frazer stick shift. It had no air-conditioning, but it was large and comfortable. Quoting my grandfather, "We lit out for Hot Springs, Arkansas, and points west." Now summertime in Alabama is warm, but it's even warmer in Arkansas and Texas.

In Hot Springs, we found a boarding house, which was common before large motels came along. Again, there was no air-conditioning in that boarding house. We had a very routine breakfast at the boarding house. The food was served at big round tables with a lazy Susan and everyone sat around and partook. After breakfast we were off to the bathhouses, where Daddy Hall would enjoy the revitalization of a hot mineral soaking. After that we usually visited the train and bus stations, where Daddy Hall loved to sit and observe the actions of the people passing through. There were all types of people to observe, of course, and I can still hear him chuckling quietly as he watched the people come and go without saying much of anything at all. After a while he would stand and say, "Let's go." That was his daily entertainment, and we spent the rest of the day just talking and enjoying fellowship.

We said goodbye to Hot Springs and continued our trek across Arkansas and Texas to the big city of Dallas, then on to the small rural area west of Fort Worth. Our plan was to visit a distant cousin of Daddy Hall's, and I remember that we had a difficult time locating the farm. His cousin was at that time a sharecropper on a farm near the small town of Dennis, Texas. The house was located down a dusty little road, through a pasture gate and on down to a big white frame house with chickens running loose in the grassless yard. The people were distant relatives of the Pinion side of his family.

When we arrived, he said, "This house looks pretty rough. Let me do the talking; if we don't like it we will leave." When the door opened we were warmly welcomed and soon found that although the people were poor, they were happy to see us and made us feel very welcome. The hospitality was cordial and genuine. We sat down to supper that evening at a large round table with an impressive lazy Susan in the middle. The lazy Susan was rotating around the center of the table with all kinds of fine, home-grown food, including hot cornbread, butterbeans, side meat, and a little bit of just about everything you could expect in a good home-cooked meal.

The house had no electricity and no running water, therefore no inside plumbing or bathroom. The outhouse, if used at night, required a lantern to see. There was a large wood-burning stove in the kitchen. The only light was provided by a kerosene lamp that sat in the center of that large table. We had an enjoyable time there before going on to another location in Texas.

Next we visited some of Daddy Hall's relatives in the small, rural community of Itasca, Texas. There was relatively little traffic on the road as we drove toward Itasca, so I asked Daddy Hall if I could drive. I was fifteen and Mother had allowed me to drive some. Daddy Hall looked at me and said, "Can you drive?" I told him that I could, and he stopped the car and changed seats with me. I slipped behind the wheel, put the car in low gear and released the clutch, and we were off and running down that dusty country road. My grandfather looked at me in surprise and said, "Had I known you could drive you could have been helping me drive all along."

A couple of his cousins suggested that we visit the stockyards at Fort Worth, and we did. After lunch I spotted a western apparel store across the street. I had never seen so much cowboy gear and I quickly spotted a pair of western boots. I really wanted those boots and finally got the man to ask my grandfather to buy them for me. Daddy Hall was always a frugal spender, and he expressed concern that I would not wear those "God Blame" boots back in Alabama. I desperately pleaded with him, but the real sale came from his cousins, who convinced him to turn loose the $12 for the boots. They were well-made boots, and I wore them back in Alabama for a long time. I still have those old Acme boots today, over 60 years later, and could never part with such a treasure. They are important to me because they remind me of my grandfather, who was a treasure himself.

Daddy Hall was a stable influence during my early development. I didn't fully realize just how influential he was until I became an adult, when I could reflect on all the time we spent together and truly understand just how much love for each other was shared. I still wish he were here today, and I wish that everyone could have an influential person like Daddy Hall in his or her life. He made a lot of difference in my life, but the biggest thing that he shared with me was a mutual love that transcends all else in our lives.

I thank God for my grandparents, my mother, my father, and all the people who had a positive influence in my life. I credit them with the success that I've had, but most of all, I thank my God. Without the help of the Lord Jesus Christ in my life, I know without a doubt that I would have fallen short of things that I did accomplish in life. God gave me the strength, the ability, and the desire to persevere to accomplish my goals in life. Those are the qualities one must cling to. One must always work toward perfection and try to become a better person.

Hall Grandparents
(Mary and Virgil)
(Mama Hall and Daddy Hall)

Mama Hall

My Grandmother Hall was born Mary Johns on September 15, 1886. She married my grandfather Virgil Gaston Hall on December 23, 1906, and was a loving wife and mother to her husband and four daughters, and a wonderful grandmother to five grandchildren.

Mama Hall had other loves in her life, also. She loved RC Cola on crushed ice. I generally made my runs each morning to Griffin's Drug Store, which was just across the street, to get her favorite treat. I entered the drug store through the back door and proceeded to the fountain, where I presented my grandmother's empty rooster goblet to Mr. Griffin. Mr. Griffin filled the goblet with crushed ice and RC Cola, and I was on my way back home. Grandmother Hall also enjoyed a dip of Rooster snuff, which she had in her lip most of the time. My cousin Jimmy Barnes said on several occasions that "Aunt Mary could spit all the way across the hog wire fence in the yard." Not only did Mama Hall love her snuff; she could consume half of a red watermelon at a single sitting.

Mama Hall rose very early in the morning and worked hard all day long. In the early years she worked at the store with my grandfather.

Later on, raising four girls that were born quite close together was pretty much a full-time job. But each day she would rise, prepare breakfast for the family, then start on lunch, and God knows how many people my grandfather would bring home for lunch, with traveling salesmen and the like passing through town. My grandmother never had one cross word to say about the visitors coming to lunch.

Generally, in the evening we would have leftovers from a large lunch. At times we would have company, and Grandmother Hall would again prepare a large meal in the evening. I remember quite well one evening meal that she prepared especially for my grandfather. It seems that he had a hankering for a fat, juicy possum dinner covered with sweet potatoes and baked in the oven. Now I knew about possums, and I did not perceive them to be that tasty. However, my grandfather said if you kept possum pinned up for a couple weeks and fed them they were good and clean. I was happy to take his word for it, but that evening he insisted that I try some of that greasy possum and I did. I can't say that I enjoyed it; I can only say I tried it and that was enough.

Mama Hall suffered from acute diabetes and high blood pressure. Her doctors urged her to lay off the salt-cured ham and homemade butter and biscuits loaded with molasses. She trusted the doctors and their diagnosis, but the biscuits and great-tasting syrup won out. She always found time to get out around the wash pot in the yard, boiling the water, doing the wash and hanging the clothes on the fence or clothesline. She might also be seen chasing down a chicken to cook for the evening meal. She worked hard and complained very little about the duties life had dealt her. She was visiting her sister, Lucy Clements, when she suffered a stroke. She was brought home and died a few days later. Her death was premature for all of us, particularly my grandfather. She passed away on April 21, 1945, just a few months short of her 59th birthday.

I was the only one of five grandchildren that my grandfather ever gave a spanking. The spanking was well justified, even in my own eyes. Mama Hall asked me to take out some trash, and I informed her that taking out the trash was woman's work. My grandfather was present and immediately set the record straight. I never again was disrespectful to my Mama Hall. He got my attention and that endured for a lifetime.

Daddy Hall had a difficult time coping with life after my grandmother's death. I spent many hours and days with him in 1947 and 1948 and noticed that he was visibly depressed. He obviously missed the companionship of his beloved wife and the wise counsel she provided.

On our final trip to Hot Springs, Arkansas, then on to Texas in 1948, I observed that he was struggling with life. I mentioned this to my mother, and my grandfather agreed to see a psychiatrist soon afterward. The doctor reported to the family his concerns for my grandfather's health. The doctor said, "I have never experienced anyone else with such deep-rooted depression." His life was empty. His wife—the mother of his children, his business partner and confidante—had left him behind and he simply could no longer cope.

On September 17, 1948, while visiting with his daughter Ruby Skinner and her husband in Tuscaloosa, he ended his life with a self-inflicted gunshot wound. He finally filled the void that existed in his life by joining my grandmother in Pleasant Hill Cemetery and in heaven. He left a monumental vacuum for those of us who remained. I will always be grateful for his love and the many lessons he taught me about life.

Near Tragedy at the Theater

My childhood was much like any other boy in a small, rural town in the South during the Great Depression. Family and friends were our most precious possessions.

My brother Joe was born at home on Sunday morning, November 10, 1935, while I attended Sunday school at Berry Baptist Church with Uncle Bill and Aunt Meryl Jones. Joe became special to me through the years, as did my cousins Billy Jones, Marion Skinner, and Paul Dobbs. Distant cousin Jimmy Barnes and close friends J. C. Shepherd and T. A. Simpson rounded out my group of close friends and playmates. Although a small town of a few hundred people during those difficult times did not offer a lot for youngsters to do, we did have a theater where we all enjoyed cowboy or Tarzan movies on Saturday evenings. Our usual Saturday night at the movies was interrupted by tragedy on November 1, 1941, when the Berry Theater caught fire and threatened the lives of approximately 200 people in attendance.

I was eight years old at the time, and Joe was five. We were seated together near the front of the theater, as close to the screen as we could get as usual, along with Jimmy Barnes, T. A.

Simpson, J. C. Shepherd, and most of our other friends.

The fire was created as a result of the highly volatile movie film combined with the extreme heat of the magnesium-powered light used to project the movie. The film literally exploded, and the flames spread rapidly. The projection booth was supposed to be fireproof; however, the projectionist panicked when the fire started and jumped from the booth to the floor below, forgetting to close the door and allowing the fire to quickly spread throughout the theater.

As people in the back of the theater started screaming, those of us in the front jumped up to see what the commotion was about and immediately saw the smoke and flames pouring from the projection room. Everyone in the theater immediately began screaming and pushing each other toward the exits. I joined in the rush and made my way out of the theater, losing sight of Joe in the smoke and panic. When I reached the street I found my mother frantically searching for her two boys. I emerged safely, however Joe was nowhere to be seen. We had become separated in the smoke and fire. I received a warm embrace from my mother as a mass of anxious people frantically searched for their loved ones who were yet to be located.

It was a cool November evening, and the flames grew higher and higher in the sky as the fire quickly spread to adjoining structures. I felt a real sinking feeling as I realized I had left my brother in that inferno ,and the thought ran through my mind, "What if Joe doesn't survive the fire?" I was too young to fully understand the full impact of what such a loss would mean to me, but I did let my mind recall November 10, 1935, when my little brother came into this world and how happy I was for that blessing. I know now what it would have meant had I lost him. I would have been deprived of a brother and my best friend.

Then I saw Charles Moore coming from the rear of the theater. My mother saw him, too, and as he appeared, he had Joe on his shoulders. My mother ran and embraced Charles then cuddled five-year-old Joe in her arms, sobbing with joy and relief. Charles shared his memory of that night with me in 2013. He said that he had been sitting close to Joe and me that night because my dad, who was living in Birmingham at the time but was in Berry that weekend, had instructed Charles, who was only 13, to keep an eye on Joe and me, and he did just that.

When the fire broke out and everyone rushed for the exits in panic, Charles found Joe under a seat, pulled him out, sat him on his shoulders, and headed out through the rear of the theater because there was no fire in that direction. Charles said the smoke was so intense that the visibility and the ability to breathe made it difficult to reach the back doors. Charles knew the way through the building, however, because he also worked as a part-time projectionist, earning 25 cents a show. Thank goodness he wasn't on duty that night. Charles was enjoying the show that night, since as an employee he was entitled to free admission.

Charles said his friend Jess White, who was sitting with him in the theater, was the real hero of the night. Jess always carried a pistol because he was a part-time deputy sheriff, and as the crowd rushed toward the double back door of the theater in panic, they discovered the door had been padlocked. Normally the door was closed and latched so that people could not enter without paying.

Jess quickly pulled his revolver from his holster, fired a single shot into the ceiling to get the attention of the screaming crowd and then pushed his way to the door, where he shot the lock off the door and allowed the frightened crowd to pour out of the theater amid the screams and smoke.

Charles said that he never considered himself a hero, but I let him know that I and all my family surely did because he risked his life that night to help save Joe and others from a burning inferno. Not a single life was lost and no one was seriously injured, thanks to Charles, Jess, and others who were never recognized.

That night was among the most frightening moments of my life. I can still hear and see the huge fire that ignited and burned an entire block of Berry, including my grandfather's mercantile store, V. G. Hall and Company; the theater; Moore's Grocery, operated by Mel and Ebelene Moore; a shooting gallery operated by Earl James, whose sons Bobby and Preston were in the theater when the fire broke out; a defunct Ford Motor Company location; and several other buildings.

A newspaper account of the incident said three people were injured when they were trampled by the crowd during the panic. Luckily, no one was killed. Police chief Oscar Davis was quoted in the newspaper as estimating the damage at $400,000.

Another near tragedy occurred during mid-summer a couple of years later, when I was about 10 years old, and it involved my good friend T. A. Simpson. T. A. and I were among a group of several boys swimming at Shepherd's Pond northeast of town when someone suggested racing across the pond and back. Everyone jumped in and swam frantically, splashing their way across the pond and back. As we returned to shore, we heard T. A. calling for help as he struggled helplessly in the middle of the pond. George Houston Martin, one of the older boys in the group at about 15 years old, quickly jumped in, swam ou,t and pulled T. A. back to shore. T. A. said years later that he had given up and would surely have drowned if George had not rescued him.

One somewhat amusing event occurred in about 1939 when a small circus, made up primarily of a few docile caged animals, stopped in town. My Uncle Conrad Dobbs, after consuming a large amount of moonshine, proclaimed that he could pet the caged lion. Uncle Con, who was in his 30s at the time, did have a special way with animals, especially dogs, and he was undaunted by what he considered nothing more than an oversized cat, especially with several of his equally inebriated buddies egging him on.

Uncle Con boldly stepped up to the cage to pet what appeared to be an old, bored and half-dozing lion. As Uncle Con reached through the bars for an intended gentle stroke of the cat's mane, the lion quickly snapped at his hand, taking the tip of a finger off his right hand. It was a sobering moment for Uncle Conrad and quickly ended his evening of shenanigans.

Despite the occasional scares, summers in Berry usually meant long days of fun and adventure. With school out, we had time to ride our horses and swim in Cedar Creek from early until late on days that seemed almost endless.

Seeking Greener Pastures

My father moved to Birmingham in 1940, feeling that more employment opportunities might be available there due to increasing military production, coupled with the fact that Birmingham was much larger than Berry. He moved in with his sister and brother-in-law and soon found work driving a truck, making local deliveries in and around Birmingham for Associated Grocers. His brother Leland and Leland's wife Lillian also lived in Birmingham. Time passed and Dad did not send for us.

Following the fire in Berry and the declaration of war with Japan and Germany several weeks later, Mother became concerned that Dad, although 33 years old and the father of two children, would be drafted into the Army. She felt that if we were living with him he might avoid the draft. Mother appealed to Dad's draft board, but when they inquired into the family support, Mother would not falsify her response. The draft board eventually determined that Dad was not sufficiently contributing to our support and sent him a notice of induction.

Mel Moore, who operated a grocery store in Berry until the November 1, 1941 theater fire destroyed his business, had moved his family to Wylam, Alabama, a suburb of Birmingham, and opened a small neighborhood grocery store. Mrs. Moore and my mother had been friends in high school and had worked together in Berry. She encouraged Mother to move to Birmingham and even offered us a place to live. We packed what few belongings we had on Daddy Hall's stake-bodied truck, and an employee of his drove Mother, Joe and me to Wylam. We unloaded the beds and a small table and four chairs. I can't recall there being much other furniture in our little two-room efficiency apartment attached to the rear of Mr. Moore's store.

The Moore family lived in a duplex attached to the store on the other side. There was a small coal-burning heater in the center of the main room, which served as the kitchen, dining room and living room of our apartment. This was the only device to prepare meals and heat the area. Mother was determined that we would survive and force Dad to assume his responsibilities. Mr. and Mrs. Moore, whose daughter Jamelle later became Alabama's First Lady as the wife of former governor James E. "Big Jim" Folsom, welcomed us as though we were family.

I feared, even as a young boy, that attempting to force my dad to live up to his family obligations might be just wishful thinking, and it was. He endured the burden for only a few weeks before becoming antsy again and looking for a place to hide. The hiding place that he selected turned out to be quite dangerous. He first approached the Marines to volunteer for service in World War II. The Marines rejected him due to high blood pressure, but that didn't deter him. He somehow managed to lower his blood pressure within a few weeks, and the Army inducted him. He was free of us again.

He was sent to basic training and later to swamp maneuvers in Louisiana and desert maneuvers in California. If he came home at all, it was only a couple of times and he was there for only a day or two. He shipped out and served until the end of the war in the South Pacific, seeing action in the Philippines, Guam and Okinawa.

While Dad was in the military, Mother, Joe and I moved from Wylam to Sylacauga, where we lived with Aunt Ruby and Uncle Edgar Skinner, who was employed at a plant at Childersburg. When Uncle Edgar was drafted into the Army we moved back to Berry to live with my grandparents. Through thick and thin, Daddy Hall and Mama Hall were always there for us.

Roy, Mother, Joe

Early Business Ventures

I think it was in 1943 that Mother, Joe and I moved back to Berry while my dad was in the Army during World War II. Money was scarce for everyone, and we were always looking for something to do to earn a little income to buy hamburgers and soda pop on Saturday afternoons.

I got with my cousin Jimmy Austin Barnes, my brother Joe, and my mother, and we talked about a business venture that we could all get into and make a little money. That business venture turned out to be a newspaper route. The route available was delivering the *Birmingham Post* newspaper. The newspapers would arrive by train or bus on a daily basis, and we would then deliver them to people's homes in town. Jimmy and I had been able to buy us a couple of new bicycles. They were really handsome bikes, equipped with knee action on the front, lights and fancy paint jobs—something very special. Joe, however, was reluctant and a little too young to work, so mother acquired a used but still nice bicycle for him.

Mother, Jimmy, Joe and I would gather in the afternoon as the papers came in to fold them and have them ready for delivery to people's homes. Normally we would walk up and place the papers on the porches, but we soon came up with what we thought was a better idea. We decided to fold the papers in the form of a square so we could throw them onto the porches from the yard, keeping us from having to walk up to the porches and thus saving a lot of steps on the route.

Well, that didn't last very long. We sailed a few papers onto roofs and damaged a couple of screen doors, and our customers quickly became unhappy with that style of delivery. So we went back to taking the papers onto the porches and even placing them behind screen doors whenever possible. This style of delivery became a hallmark as people recognized the quality of service they were getting from their paper carriers. There was one particular lady on the route who said that we were the nicest people in the world because we always brought her paper up to the front door. I delivered the paper to this lady, but Jimmy Barnes somehow took credit for this compliment, or at least that's what my mother always said.

The next challenge we faced was collecting money owed us for the newspapers. Every Saturday we would go around town and collect for the past week's newspapers. This was a must in order for us to pay our own newspaper bill. I remember one person in particular who always gave us a hard time about paying his bill. That person was my Grandmother Hall's brother-in-law Will Barnes, who was actually Jimmy Barnes' grandfather. I always referred to Will Barnes affectionately as Uncle Will, but without question every week he would argue and hold out, refusing to pay his bill until his wife, who I called Aunt Ruth because she was my grandmother Hall's sister, came to our defense. "Will Barnes, you pay those boys what you owe them; end of discussion," she would say, and Uncle Will would reluctantly hand over our money.

The paper route didn't last forever, but despite our minor problems it was a time in my life that was very meaningful, and it taught us all many valuable lessons, including responsibility. The income was nice, but I discovered that the most important thing was to make sure the customers got their newspapers and that they were pleased with the service. What I learned in that job was that there is no substitute for service, and I have never forgotten it. We also learned to manage and save our money and the importance of utilizing our time wisely. It also gave us the confidence and momentum to proceed into other adventures, and I went on to experience several other opportunities to be an entrepreneur.

Soon after giving up our paper route, Jimmy and I became joint owners of a cattle business, although we were only about 10 or 12 years old at the time. Using money we earned

working in the fields for Jimmy's father Joe
Pete Barnes, we purchased some five or six
calves for $5 to $7 dollars each. We pastured the
calves in Uncle Bill Jones' pasture near the
Jotemdown grocery store on Tuscaloosa Avenue
on the south side of town. The store was
operated by my great uncle Abner Hall and his
wife Jinnie and got its name from a popular
radio show of the era whose characters "Lum"
and "Abner" operated a fictional "Jotemdown"
grocery store.

Jimmy and I intended to fatten our calves
up and sell them for a nice profit. We thought
we knew what it was all about. We knew the
business world and what we should do, but it's
difficult to make decisions at that age.

I particularly remember one big purchase
we made. Jim and I were looking at a big bull
calf owned by Dr. David Wright, one of two
local medical doctors in Berry. The calf was
quite nice looking, and we asked Dr. Wright if
he would sell it to us. He agreed to the sale, and
we paid him $10 for what we thought was quite
a handsome white bull calf. We felt confident
our deal would yield a large profit. As we led
the calf down the road toward our pasture,
however, we began to more closely examine it
and noticed that the calf's skin was adhering
tightly to his rib cage. We became more alarmed
and worried about our investment by the
moment as we encouraged that calf to move

down the road. We thought we just might be out our $10.

Fear gripped our bodies as Jimmy and I continued to examine the calf and talk about our investment as we walked along that dusty, hot road in the summertime. We knew that on the way to our pasture we would pass Mr. Clell Ray's cattle barn, so we stopped by Mr. Ray's barn and asked him if he'd be interested in buying our calf. All we wanted for it was the $10 we had in it.

Mr. Ray paused for a moment and said, "Boys. I don't know if that calf is worth $10." I looked at Jimmy and Jimmy looked at me, both thinking that we had made a mistake that time. Then Mr. Ray said, "I will bail you boys out and give you the $10." We took the money and went on our merry way, thinking that we had made a good deal by getting our money back. When I reached my grandfather Hall's home he asked us about the calf. Jimmy and I told him that we had gotten the calf but that its hide was growing to his rib cage and we were worried about that so we sold it to Mr. Ray and recovered our money. My grandfather looked at us and said, "Boys, did you not understand that you could have pulled that hide every day and it would have loosened up and that calf would have grown and you would have had a fine investment?" We quickly realized that we weren't the cattle barons we thought we were, so we promptly sold all our calves for a small profit and moved on.

Many times when we are faced with adversity or with a situation that we don't know how to handle the easy way is to bail out just as Jimmy and I did. We did recover our investment, but as the years passed and other opportunities manifested themselves, I realized that the decision I made then was probably not the wisest one. It was another valuable learning experience, however, and it would help me and encourage me to make better decisions in the coming years.

Daddy Hall came up with another idea for me to earn a little money in the spring of 1944. One evening at supper, in his matter-of-fact way, he said, "Roy, it's time for you to learn a little about farming, get to know what most of my customers do every day. My boy, I want you to plant cotton on that acre of ground I have around the corner. I want you to plow the ground, plant the seeds, tend to crop during the growing season, then harvest it, bale it, and sell it."

Of course I agreed to do it. I did anything Daddy Hall suggested and was excited about the chance to earn some money. I even thought it might be fun, and it was for a while—a very short while. It didn't take long for me to realize that cotton farming was hard work.

Daddy Hall provided a mule to break the ground and got one of his sharecroppers, a tall thin black man known as "Legs," to do most of the really hard ground-breaking work, but I was there through every step of the process from beginning to end. I learned to chop cotton, wearing blisters in my tender hands with the rough hoe handle in the process. I thought plowing the mule would be fun, but I soon learned otherwise when I stepped behind one of the orneriest creatures ever known to man.

Legs helped with the planting of the cotton, and a few weeks later came the chopping and the weeding. Most of the time, more than one cotton plant came up in each hill and the sprouts would be too close together to allow any of them to develop into a strong plant. My task was to examine the grouping carefully and meticulously remove the weakest plants and shore-up the remaining ones by pulling more dirt around the stalk. As I thinned the cotton, I also had to remove the weeds that were trying to suck the limited moisture and nutrients away from the plants. A couple of more plowings were required to keep the weeds down before the cotton was "laid by" and left to grow, bloom and mature in the hot summer sun.

Finally, in October, not long after I started sixth grade, the cotton bolls opened up and the pure white cotton glistened in the bright autumn sun. It was time to reap the rewards of my labor.

Although I had help from my mother and my brother Joe, I soon learned that picking cotton was a major chore and the most laborious of all of the tasks I had undertaken so far. My cousin Marion Skinner helped briefly with the picking, but gave it up after collecting a whopping two pounds. That canvas cotton sack grew heavier and heavier as I filled it and dragged it up and down the rows by a strap around my neck and shoulder. It was far from easy, but I believed it was the last of a long line of tasks leading up to my cash reward.

We finally loaded the cotton onto a wagon that was hitched to a pair of mules and hauled it the short distance down Dobbs Avenue to Daddy Hall's cotton gin, where the seeds from the cotton fibers were removed and the cotton compressed into two 640-pound bales. It was not a bad harvest for a single acre.

I proudly took my cotton samples to Daddy Hall and blurted out, "Here's my cotton, you can pay me now," fully expecting immediate cash. I was surprised when Daddy Hall responded, "Boy, you go get price quotes from Shepherd's and Theron Cannon." These two purchased a lot of local cotton, although Daddy Hall probably brokered a lot more than they did. "Are you going with me?" I asked. "No," he replied. "You are on your own." I may have been only 12 years old, but I had previous business experience.

With my samples tucked under my arm, I walked slowly up the street to Shepherd's and then to Theron Cannon's, on my way to getting price quotes as Daddy Hall suggested. I didn't fully understand what was going on. I wondered why Daddy Hall sent me to them when he could have bought the cotton himself, but I didn't question him about it.

Shepherd offered 18 cents a pound, and when Theron Cannon offered me 20 cents a pound, which was higher than the going rate, I quickly took it. Clutching the money tightly and with a wide grin on my face, I ran all the way back to Daddy Hall's, eager to tell him of my shrewd bargaining skills. When I told him I had sold the cotton, he said, in words that were his way of getting my attention, "Ay, God, boy, I just wanted you to get a quote, not sell your cotton."

The way Daddy Hall spoke to me caught my mother by surprise and she quickly came to my defense. "Papa, he asked you to go with him and you said no. You should have gone and helped him. This is done and don't you ever mention it again!" Later I realized that Daddy Hall would have paid me more than either of the other two cotton dealers in town but he wanted me to learn the value of my work and a little about business. He wanted me to understand how the free market system works, and thus introduced me to the world of producing, marketing, bargaining and sales—all skills that would serve me well later in life.

My grandfather Hall was a wise man, but his expectations of a 12 year old were a little too high at times. I was grateful for all the lessons he taught me in my short time I was with him; however, he passed away in 1948, certainly much too prematurely. There was so much more that I could have gleaned from Daddy Hall that I was deprived of. I am thankful for those valuable lessons he taught me, and I will forever be grateful.

Dad Returns from War

The United States was massing troops on every island in the Pacific in 1945, preparing for a land invasion of mainland Japan in a battle that would surely have meant death for hundreds of thousands of soldiers on both sides. My dad and thousands of other GIs were staged on the Japanese island of Okinawa, which had been taken by the Allies at the cost of 12,000 American and 100,000 Japanese lives.

Harry S. Truman became president of the United States in April 1945 following the sudden death of Franklin D. Roosevelt, and in August 1945 he decided to use a top-secret weapon—the atomic bomb, which was still in the experimental stages—in an attempt to force Japan to surrender. The deployment of two atomic bombs, one on Hiroshima and the other on Nagasaki, Japan, killed scores of thousands of Japanese civilians but helped end the war within two weeks and preserve the lives of possibly an even greater number of American and allied military personnel.

I was thankful to learn soon after the Japanese surrender on August 14, 1945, that my father had survived the fighting in the Pacific and was on his way home. He departed Okinawa in October 1945 and landed one month later at

Fort Lewis, Washington. There he was transported on a makeshift troop train with a number of other GIs and sent to Camp Shelby, Mississippi. On his trip across the county, Dad met a young airman who had also been in the Pacific area. They had known each other in earlier days in Berry.

The man was Elmer Lawson, affectionately known as "Runt" due to his small stature. I recently talked to Mr. Lawson, who, on October 10, 2013, turned 104 years old and lives in Boley, not far from Berry. He was on the same troop ship returning from Okinawa as my dad. Mr. Lawson's recollection of those days in 1945 was as clear as if they had happened yesterday. He said that he and my father sailed for a month across the Pacific to Fort Lewis, Washington. Mr. Lawson said he spotted my dad on the crowded ship but did not speak to him and renew their old friendship until they later met in the Post Exchange at Fort Lewis.

Dad and Mr. Lawson mustered out at Camp Shelby on December 11, 1945. Anxious to get back to Fayette County, they pooled their money with another soldier and hired a taxi at Camp Shelby to drive them to Fayette County with a stop in Columbus, Mississippi, to deposit the third soldier. I recently talked with Mr. Lawson, and he said that he and Dad picked up some whiskey on the way home. I inquired if it was moonshine whiskey, and Mr. Lawson said it wasn't. Mr. Lawson said he opened his bottle and took a little drink but didn't like the taste, so he didn't drink it. I imagine my dad consumed both bottles, however. The cab finally dropped Mr. Lawson off near Fayette, where he lived about three miles out of town between Berry and Fayette at that time. Dad came on to Berry, arriving back home safe and sound on December 12, 1945.

On Veterans Day 2012 I had an opportunity to talk with Mr. Lawson at the Veterans Day ceremony at Berry Elementary School, where veterans from all wars were honored. Mr. Lawson was the elder statesman among us all at 103 years old. He was a little feeble, but his memory was fantastic. He and I reminisced about his memories of World War II and his and Dad's taxi ride home. "Runt" Lawson died suddenly January 16, 2014, at age 104. He was laid to rest January 18, 2014, which was my 81st birthday.

After my dad returned from the war we talked some about his experiences, but only when he had consumed an ample supply of booze to loosen his tongue. I am sure it was difficult to talk about some of the situations the GIs encountered throughout the Pacific in battles for such islands as the Philippines, Okinawa and Guam. Dad's wartime experiences didn't dampen his desire for alcohol. I suppose it would even be fair to assume that the horrors of war contributed to his drinking, and maybe so, but I suspect the desire for whiskey he acquired at the age of 12 was the real factor.

We all thought things might be different this time; we felt sure that the war had made Dad realize the value of his family. And it did seem better for a little while, but it was short lived. It wasn't long before Dad returned to his same drinking routine.

We moved out of my grandparents' home and rented a room in the home of Mrs. Essie Johnson, which was located on Highway 18, just a couple of blocks from Daddy Hall's house. Aunt Essie's house was blessed with a huge yard covered with green grass, which provided an ideal spot for our football games. The afternoons of January 1946 usually found me, Joe, Jimmy Barnes, and other youngsters from town choosing sides and playing football.

I recall the big heroes of the day were The University of Alabama players Harry Gilmer and Rebel Steiner. Jimmy would always play the role of Gilmer, leaping high in the air and throwing the ball as I streaked down the field to catch the pass. Those were good old days in Berry, but unfortunately they were coming to an end.

My dad again became restless and expressed the need to move on. He went to Birmingham, where he found work, and we soon followed. We said goodbye to our family and friends in Berry and began our final trek to Birmingham.

Mother was Our Breadwinner

When Mother, Joe and I joined Dad in Birmingham, we purchased a modest home in the West End area of Birmingham, and Joe and I enrolled at Stonewall Jackson Elementary School.

My mother, then 40 years old, having long ago realized that she would always be the family breadwinner, applied for employment with Sears Roebuck and Company at a brand-new store that had just opened on First Avenue and 14th Street. She was immediately hired and worked there for 25 years until she was required to take retirement at age 65. I believe she would never have left Sears had there not been a compulsory age to retire at that time. Her work and the peace she enjoyed at Sears gave her a feeling of security.

My dad had secured a job as a welder's apprentice with Birmingham Ornamental Iron Works on the G.I. Bill. He said the welding bothered his eyes so badly that he could not continue that pursuit.

My mother wanted so badly for my dad to succeed that she financed two businesses for him to no avail as the drinking led to disaster in both instances. She realized she would be the financial support for the family.

After working all day at Sears, she would come home tired, only to be the recipient of continuous verbal abuse from my father, who followed her around all evening cursing her for no reason at all. This went on almost nightly until my father finally had too much to drink or just got too tired and fell asleep. There was one thing for sure, if he had a dollar, it went to buy a drink. The same thing happened again and again because he always found a way to get a drink of liquor whether he had the money or had to mooch off someone else. He would share a bottle with anyone, and it didn't matter who.

The constant cursing and verbal abuse my mother was receiving became intolerable. I often said to myself that if I hated anyone that much I would not stay around, but then I realized that my mother was the provider and the stability for our family, and that my dad did need somewhere to eat and sleep.

One evening as always, my dad was drunk and following my mother around relentlessly cursing, "GD this" and "GD that," with most of his abuse directed toward her church work. My dear mother was exhausted from working all day and now she must spend the evening in tears until my dad finally went to sleep.

I recall one evening in particular. I had heard my dad curse and carry on until it was more than I could take, and it was more than mother could take. She was in tears. I wrestled my dad to the floor in our kitchen and as I held a butcher knife to his throat, I told him if he didn't stop this verbal abuse on my mother I would kill him. My sweet mother pulled me away, and I'm grateful for that. A child should never be provoked to that degree of anger, and I never was again. Did the abuse cause pain? Certainly it did. My dad never changed until the last year of his life. I will share his final story a little later.

By the time I reached high school I realized that I should assume more responsibility around the house in order to help my mother. I began to cook and prepare our evening meals to give her a few moments of free time or rest that she so deserved. My mother enjoyed high school football games and just going out sometimes to get away from all the abuse at home. In the final years of my dad's life he did share something with me, and it was something for which my mother had prayed for a long time. I will share it because I feel it is a paramount issue in my dad's life.

Dad contracted melanoma cancer that spread to his brain, affecting his eyesight. When he was eventually struck by the disease, Mother and I were by his side in the emergency room of the hospital. Dad's eyes were set. There was no movement whatsoever in his body. I looked at Mother and said, "I believe dad is gone." Later he shared something with me and only me as far as I know. It was on a Sunday morning when I was sitting with him at home. I had agreed to stay home so Mother could attend Lakeside Baptist Church, which she loved so dearly. Dad's eyesight was almost gone. He now was transformed from a belligerent alcoholic to a thoughtful man with only a short time to live.

He said, "Son, I remember you and Mother with me in the hospital. I could hear you, but I couldn't speak or move any part of my body. What I am going to share with you today no one would believe, but that's okay because I believe it. When I was at death's door, God made an appearance. He let me see heaven and hell. He presented hell first, and the Bible or no account could picture anything so horrific or so bad. Then God let me observe heaven, and it was more magnificent, more glorious than anyone could ever describe. I knew then that I could not choose hell. I chose to be with God in heaven," he said.

"If I were to live for any given time, I would never take a drink of alcohol again, ever. I know I only have a few precious months at best to live, but I have now found a peace that I've never known before."

As far as I know Dad never revealed this vision even to my mother. For the next few months Mother was by Dad's side, providing all the comforts of life until he drew his final breath here on earth. At the end, he softly asked, "Mother, how much longer will it be?" Mother looked at Dad and sweetly responded, "Not very much longer now." With a smile on his face and touching Mother's hand, Dad thanked her for everything she had done for him and said, "I am now ready to go."

My dad died from the cancer on October 10, 1982. My mother passed away on September 20, 1997, after a stroke. They are buried at Pleasant Hill Cemetery in Berry, finally together for all time. I do believe that regardless of all my father's faults and insensitivity he is in heaven.

When we published my mother's account of her life, Phyllis and I entitled her book *The Living Story of Gwendolyn Hall Dobbs' Journey of Faith: A Freckle-Faced Angel.* I have no doubt that she was my angel sent from God. She gave and sustained life for me, and I will be forever grateful for her influence on my life.

I believe everyone experiences many crossroads and multiple choices in life. I know I did and still do every day. I hope this segment of my book will illuminate the path for a drifting soul. I may not be able to help or guide you, but I know someone who can. Take the hand of the

Lord Jesus Christ; He can help you through the valley of darkness and death. That's what my Dad shared with me.

The years in West End produced a mixed bag of joy and pain. Our home life was in constant flux, with Mother working and Dad constantly condemning her for her church work and her belief in God. I wondered why God would permit such verbal abuse to be levied against one of His children. When we read the account of Job in the Old Testament we can better understand. God has a purpose, and His rewards come when we complete this life and go home to be with Him. My dear mother surely earned her ticket to heaven. As the Apostle Paul said, "I have run the race and completed the course." His treasures were waiting in heaven and so were my dear mother's.

It is difficult even now to recall the relentless badgering my dad imposed upon my mother. The constant cursing and badgering of my mother took a toll on Joe and me, and we vowed that we would elevate ourselves and do something constructive with our lives. Thanks to my mother and God, we accomplished that.

Many of the accounts of my dad's life were negative; I realize that. I did love my dad, however; I just could never understand his life choices. We all are responsible for whatever path we pursue. Thank God I chose a more positive path for my life, as did my brother Joe.

Championship Football Team

I had completed elementary school with the sixth-grade class at Berry, graduating with a full ceremony. In Birmingham, I completed the seventh and eighth grades at Stonewall Jackson Elementary School (1946–1947) and again graduated from elementary school.

From 1948–1951, I attended West End High School, where I had the honor of playing on the 1949 city championship football team. West End won all of its city-wide games in 1949 and closed the season against Ramsey High in the popular Thanksgiving Day Classic at Legion Field.

As a young junior in high school, I was playing with a group of older boys with more experience. They were football players. They were not physically large compared to other teams in the city but they had a great deal of spirit and a tenacious attitude to win. Approximately 12 of the 35 members of the 1949 team attended a 60th anniversary reunion just a couple of years ago. I shared with them my thoughts and recollections of the 1949 championship team. I expressed a genuine thanks to all of the remaining team members. I was not a star player, but I was a part of that team victory. The 1949 West End team members demonstrated the epitome of what in later years I understood as true teamwork. The under-sized group of young men exhibited a keen desire to emerge as champions.

We played the championship game on Thanksgiving Day, 1949. We were picked by the Birmingham News to lose to Ramsey, a much larger and probably more experienced team. However, at the end of the game, due to the determination to play our hearts out, the West End Lions came out victorious. I later realized how little I contributed to the team's victory, but I will always cherish the experience of being a member of a championship team.

Looking back, I am confident that I could have elevated my contributions to the team, even though it might not have made a difference to anyone except me. Still, the experience was another building block on my road to success. I possessed the talent, but I lacked the commitment to excellence. Though my mother encouraged me, my dad was seldom there to encourage or to help me realize my potential. We all need someone to encourage us and at times give us a little nudge.

This book is dedicated to that premise that we all can rise above mediocrity. Hopefully, some of my words will challenge readers to push themselves, realize the deep-down talents that everyone has, and strive to be the very best that one can be. There are hidden talents in each and every one of us not yet manifested.

Perhaps this memory will serve as an example of what I mean. I was in Montgomery, Alabama, in 1952 to watch West End High School play Sidney Lanier High in a football game. My brother Joe was a running back for West End, and Bart Starr was quarterback for Sidney Lanier. West End was mauled that evening and Starr later went on to play at The University of Alabama, where he played on a team that had a losing season; however, Bart signed a professional contract with the Green Bay Packers. He ended up in the Pro Football Hall of Fame.

Joe, by the way, went on to earn a degree in electrical engineering at The University of Alabama. He worked for Alabama Power Company and McGraw-Edison for a short time before moving to Robertsdale, Alabama, where he worked for many years before retirement. Joe lives in Foley today with his second wife Joyce, and we frequently chat face-to-face on the computer via Skype.

Vince Lombardi, the great coach of the Green Bay Packers, saw something in Starr that had not yet been developed—a hidden talent. Starr became one of the best and most talented quarterbacks to ever play in the National Football League. It just took someone to help

Starr realize his full potential, and Lombardi was known for having that ability.

We all have hidden talents; some are just reluctant to seek them out. Hopefully this will prompt someone to realize those hidden talents and seek to perform at a higher level. We should ask ourselves if we are performing at our very highest level and be honest with ourselves in doing so. It has been repeatedly drilled into us to reach for the gold, be the best we can be, but that's what life is really all about—striving to be the very best that we can in whatever we do. Gratification comes not just in reaching the top, but also by enjoying the trip to the top.

Roy Dobbs
(West End High School)
(Sophomore Year, 1948)

Injury Opens a New Door

Springtime in high school meant it was time to roll out for spring football practice at West End High School, and that was the case in 1950. We were in the middle of the first week and everything was going well when all at once I experienced a sharp pain in my lower back. Coach Proctor, our head coach, felt it was just a strain and taped up my back and asked me to continue with our workouts and training. It was most difficult to do as the pain was excruciating. Each day the pain grew worse. Finally, I informed Coach Proctor that I had to go to the doctor. He agreed, and I went to a bone specialist regarding the pain in the lower part of my back.

The diagnosis was a fractured vertebra, a dissolved disk, and a pinched nerve where the two vertebrae rubbed against each other. The situation was rather acute because my spine was slipping apart. Dr. Ralph Terhune, a prominent surgeon in Birmingham, suggested that we fuse the lower part of my back. He gave me the option that I could probably wear a brace, take medication, and maybe delay the surgery. To me, corrective surgery was the most feasible alternative. I wanted some immediate relief and was certainly looking at the long-range also. I opted for a spinal fusion.

The doctor explained that he would take part of the shinbone out of my left leg and place it into my back with two silver screws. I entered the hospital with optimism. When I emerged from the operating room into my private room I found my left leg and ankle supported by a fluffy pillow. My leg was hurting so badly that I could not concentrate on my back problems. I spent two weeks flat on my back in the hospital, and when I say flat of my back, I mean with no pillow under my head and I could not turn left or right on my own. I needed the assistance of an orderly or nurse or a combination of both to turn onto my side. Those two weeks were a real ordeal.

At the end of the two-week period, which I vividly remember as though it were yesterday, the doctor said, "Let's go down and wrap a plaster cast around the lower part of your body." That procedure was quite long, and while they were finishing the last round of bandages, I was standing with pins and needles coming up from my feet up to my knees, or at least it felt that way. I finally said to the doctor, "You had better hurry up because I'm almost to the point of passing out." I survived the ordeal, and at the end of two weeks I was released from the hospital and allowed to go home again with special attention required. Wearing that cast from my chest to my hips in June, July and August was miserable.

My mother was working full time at Sears and was unable to be my attending caretaker. My dad was not around and my brother was out doing his own thing, so that only left one person to look after me. That one person was an angel in the person of my girlfriend Patsy Dickison. She fed me my meals and was there to take care of me every day in the hospital. I never forgot that even though Patsy and I broke up some months afterwards, which was probably all my fault. At least that's what my mother always told me each time I broke up with a girlfriend. Patsy was more than just a girlfriend. She was a very special person in my life, a very caring person, and I will never forget her.

Many of my friends asked me what I would do now that I could no longer play football. I had to ponder that question because I was now without a football team. The doctor had informed me that contact sports were no longer an option for me. But my friends and I knew how active I was and how I enjoyed being involved in something. One suggestion was that since I enjoyed singing, why didn't I pursue that area by taking lessons or joining a group, and I did just that.

My mother provided the financing for me to take private voice lessons under Mrs. George Roepke, who lived in West End just a short way from our house and very close to West End high school. Mrs. Roepke had been blind since she was five or six years old. She was truly an inspiration to me, not only in the area of voice training, which was excellent, but her attitude toward life was an inspiration, something that I wasn't familiar with.

She never complained or talked about what she couldn't do because she was blind, but did things in spite of her blindness. She selected the music and encouraged me to work hard to develop proper techniques. She would look up a song and write it in braille. Mrs. Roepke played the piano beautifully, and I enjoyed working with her, as she taught me a great deal. She insisted that I breathe properly, sing from my diaphragm, and open my jaw to let the music flow freely. She was not into pop or country and western music. It had to be show tunes or semi-classical music.

Over the next few months, Mrs. Roepke and I worked very hard, and we were invited to a number of civic clubs and other venues around the Birmingham area to entertain. I would drive, and Mrs. Roepke would grab my arm and I would lead her across the busy streets. She was confident that although I was only 17 years old I would take care of her. She trusted me, and I'm so grateful for that.

As we progressed in our music, someone from my school heard me sing and I was asked to perform at the high school general assembly one morning. We did a number of songs, one from the Desert Song musical and one I most vividly recall was "Old Man River," which we performed at the conclusion of our program in the auditorium without any kind of sound system, just the piano and my voice. We received a standing ovation from my high school peers. That was a thrill and a real compliment that encouraged me to continue my work and singing.

I have often thought of Mrs. Roepke and what happened to her, but as I went off to college, spent four years in the military and then a number of years in Phoenix, Arizona, I simply lost touch. Although I lost touch with her, I never lost the memory of Mrs. Roepke and what she meant in my life. I had other voice teachers and instructors in California and Arizona, but Mrs. Roepke is the person who really got me going in my singing career. She was and remains an inspiration to me in many ways.

Thanks to her training, I continued my music throughout my life. After my military days from 1953 to 1957, I lived in Phoenix from 1957–1965 and I sang at different locations. As a member of the Telephone Company Pioneers, a traveling group in the Phoenix area, we entertained at the Veterans Hospital and other places. When I was singing at Mountain Shadows Resort for the Telephone Company

Pioneers, in Scottsdale, Waylon Jennings was getting his career going at a night spot just down the street. He was getting his country-western career going hot and heavy at that time. I appreciated the fact that Waylon probably did a little bit better than I did in his singing career. However, I always questioned if that style of life were something I wished to pursue.

He may have been more successful in the country music industry than I, but was he more successful than I? By what scale do we measure success? So often we look at someone's success and fail to look at the road they might have to travel. That road can become difficult, with many curves and many potholes, and the price of success can become higher than the rewards. That's what I looked at in the music industry. It was a demanding career path, and I am thankful that I chose not to travel it. My experience in music taught me a great deal, and one of the lessons was that most rewards you receive in life come with a price.

To some the cost of performing a small job or task may present too many obstacles to overcome, potholes to avert or other unworthy demands. So often one finds him or herself being content to produce at a level that is acceptable but somewhat below what is expected. From all my experiences, I have found that the one thing that encouraged me most was to continue to strive beyond what was comfortable, to push for the goals that were a little more difficult to attain, and to expect to enjoy the results of a job well done.

Because I enjoy singing, I have continued to sing in church and in any other venue that I could find through the years. I formed a group of Southern Gospel singers consisting of my son David, Mike Ellison, who at that time was mayor of the small town of Belk, and myself. We were known as Glory Bound. Our trio sang at the local television station in Berry. You might question how a town of 1,200 people would have a Christian broadcast television station, but we did and it is still in operation today. After Mike retired from our group, we were joined by a young woman from Berry named Jennifer Handley. We changed our group's name to the Gloryheirs and sang for a number of years together at churches throughout the area. David and Jennifer eventually went out on their own singing country-western and gospel music for several years.

I remember one evening we were in a church in Fayette performing a gospel concert. Our heavy equipment was sitting on the floor. We had just broken it down and were getting ready to load it in our vehicles. My grandson A. J., who was visiting with us from Djibouti, Africa, was not talking very much at that point in his life. Standing near our group was a quite hefty gentleman somewhat younger than we were. A. J. looked up at the man and motioned for him to pick up the equipment. He didn't say pick up; he just motioned for him to pick up that heavy amplifier and with his finger pointed out to our car, and the communication was very effective. The man picked up the heavy amplifier and assisted us with the loading of our equipment. A.J. is the son of my youngest child Joe and his wife Carol, who also have a beautiful little girl named Lydia.

Just as I learned a great deal from my football days at West End High school in Birmingham, I was equally blessed with the many experiences I enjoyed being a member of the singing group or singing solo. It would have been easy for me to have just admitted defeat when I was crushed by the fact that I could no longer participate in contact sports. I could have found a valid excuse for quitting. Probably no one else cared, but I did. I was driven to reach up and pull myself out of the grip of defeat.

The important lesson that experience taught me was that you dust off yourself, even when you've been put down, even when you have been somewhat defeated, learn from the experience, and move forward with a new challenge. We are all given opportunities to excel in life. I believe that it is only when we refuse to accept those challenges in life, when we find ourselves in bitter defeat, experiencing desperation, that we just give up.

I was thinking of a story about a person who had an opportunity to make a difference in his life, and he ran from that opportunity but couldn't get away. The story took place in the Old Testament. It was in the days that God had called Jonah to go to Nineveh and preach the word of repentance to those people. Jonah did not want to do that; it was not what he had chosen for his life.

I thought about Jonah and how typical that is with many of us today. God called out to Jonah as he calls out to us today. God told him to tell the people of Nineveh that if they did not repent the wrath of God would come down. Jonah elected not to obey God's command. So often today we refuse to do those things that we know we should do because they are too difficult. The task was not one that Jonah really desired. It was too difficult and not a popular assignment, so he ran in an attempt to avoid the assignment.

Many times we, too, refuse to attack the more difficult challenges of life, choosing instead a more elementary challenge, one much more easily attainable. After much distress and running and hiding we could well discover as Jonah did that following God's command and accepting those more challenging assignments will result in greater rewards in our lives. Never settle for the easy jobs. Never settle for the insignificant accomplishments of life. The challenge is to rise above mediocrity and truly make a difference in someone else's life as well as your own.

A Real Job and My First Car

I graduated from West End High School in 1951. It was the beginning of summer, and I was feeling good about completing my 12 years of school. But with the coming of age came serious responsibilities I had not faced before. It was time for me to get a real job and try to imagine what the future held for me. I had my eye on a new, gray 1951 Studebaker Starlite coupe with a hot, V8 engine and manual transmission. The ride would surely make me a big man with the girls. A major hurdle remained, however: How would I pay for this keen ride? I sought and landed what I considered a good job. I began my work career with Butler Manufacturing Company, in Birmingham, a manufacturer of steel storage tanks and large custom steel pipe.

I purchased my car at a small Studebaker dealership located in the suburbs known as Ensley. The price was staggering at $1,939, and when you make only $35 a week, that's a pretty strong dollar figure.

At Butler Manufacturing, I was directed to the personnel and timekeeping office in the main plant. My assignment was to assist Paul Burthon, who was a graduate of Alabama

Polytechnic Institute, which later became Auburn University. Paul and I maintained the time cards for the hourly workers in the plant. Each week we calculated time and wages, using an antiquated device called a comptometer, the forerunner of the computer, I suppose. Paul was a great guy with whom to work.

Wages in 1951 were not on the same scale of today. Top welders made three dollars an hour, and I guess I made probably a dollar per hour. It was a small amount of money, but it would help pay for my car. I borrowed the money from my mother, and I was to pay her back on a monthly basis, which I did. (Well, almost. Mother said I actually repaid most of the loan.)

During my brief tenure at Butler Manufacturing Company I met Leonard Costen, who was the Comptroller. One day Leonard approached me with an attractive proposition. He had a rustic cabin on a lake near Tannehill State Park in Bessemer. He was interested in selling the cabin to purchase a nicer cabin on that same lake. The property was a closed corporation consisting of 67 acres and a nice lake. Twelve families owned their own homes, plus an equal share of the acreage. I confronted my mother with this great deal. We could buy into this association for only $2,500.

We went down to look at the rustic cabin on the lake and as my mother opened the door and looked inside her first comment was, "Papa has better looking houses for some of his share croppers." My response was that the old house had many attributes, but my mother still wasn't totally convinced. I quickly pointed out how Uncle Bill Holder and I could transform this place into a nice weekend getaway cottage. After some reluctance, my mother agreed to purchase the property for $2,500.

The property was located about 30 miles one way from our home in West End, and the highways were not what they are today. Nevertheless, with my persuasive salesmanship and my commitment to ensure the enhancements of the property would take place, my mother wrote a check to Mr. Costen for the $2,500. I felt confident that she was not 100 percent convinced that the cabin was a sound investment. However, after the renovations were completed, along with many other improvements in the area, and particularly after the day Interstate 20/59 came through, the property had gained significant additional value.

My dad and mother had a chance to enjoy the cabin many times. In the summers, they would go down and stay several months. They rented their home in Birmingham to one of the Birmingham Barons baseball players and his family each summer for several years. I do believe that was an enjoyable time in my mother's life. She spent some quality time with my dad there. The lake property experience proved to be an enjoyable one for all of us. That property investment turned out to be profitable, especially when the highway department purchased part of the property to construct the new Interstate highway between Birmingham and Tuscaloosa. Mother eventually sold the lake place for $5,000, turning a solid profit.

Korean War Changes Plans

As 1952 approached I had a strong urge to continue my formal education. I talked with Mr. Reid, plant manager at Butler Manufacturing, and he encouraged me to attend college. He expressed regrets because he felt I had a future with Butler; however, he stressed the importance of getting a college degree. That college education would take me more than the normal four years. The Korean War created a gap of 20 years, and I ultimately completed my college work at Auburn in 1972.

I entered The University of Alabama in September 1952, rooming with my old high school friend Bill Wesley. Bill and I entered ROTC together along with the basic freshman courses. Things were going well. My school work was different and somewhat more difficult from high school. I should have been more attentive to my schoolwork and probably less attentive to the female companionship. I soon fell deeply in love with Elizabeth Gary, a girl from Boaz, Alabama. Elizabeth eventually broke my heart with a "Dear John" letter while I was in the Air Force.

As Bill and I pursued ROTC, the scuttlebutt was a strong possibility we would be drafted for service in Korea, which was not an encouraging thought. None of us wanted to go to Korea to be in that war. I was confident, however, that I would not be drafted from college. I had experienced a fractured back playing football in 1950, which resulted in a spinal fusion. I felt that problem would keep me out of the military; however, I did not want to take the chance. I perceived myself to be smarter than that.

I had always heard that the Air Force had a much higher physical requirement than did the Army. I decided to take advantage of the winter break at The University and seek a physical with the Air Force. I was not anticipating leaving; I just intended to take a physical. I was certain I would be reclassified and that would keep me from being drafted into the military.

I went to the Air Force recruiting station in Birmingham and talked with the recruiting sergeant. I explained that I did not expect to be selected by his organization, but that I did want to be reclassified and therefore I needed to take a physical. The sergeant opened his desk drawer and exposed a large number of applications for the Air Force. He jokingly said, "All these applicants want to circumvent the Army draft." He quickly stated, however, that if I took the test and made a high score I could go to Montgomery the next day for a physical.

I completed the lengthy exam, and the sergeant immediately reviewed and checked my answers. His voice resonated with excitement as he said, "You are ready to go. You scored in the upper percentile." I reiterated that I was going only for a physical. "The Air Force will never take me because I have a left eye vision of 20 over 200, which cannot be corrected." I was born with amblyopia and my eyesight was much below the rigid requirements of the Air Force. I also had an ace in the hole due to my spinal fusion about 18 months earlier. I was fully confident that I would be returning to The University of Alabama for my second semester of college and to be with my fiancée Elizabeth.

After two days of physical exams with multiple doctors, I discovered (If there is a will, then there is a way.) that the need for military personnel outweighed physical defects. I soon found myself being sworn in for a four-year tour of duty with the Air Force. I was immediately deployed to Lackland Air Force Base in San Antonio, Texas, for basic training. That was the end of an era and the beginning of my first true manhood experience.

I now faced a totally new experience. I was in for nine long weeks of rigorous training, while consuming food that I had not before been used to eating. I was integrated into a squadron of people from all over the United States, from different cultures and different walks of life with different desires for their futures. Toward the end of my boot camp I ran into two old friends from Berry, J. C. Shepherd and Curry Smith. I had not seen either of them in many years. It seemed they had also enlisted in the Air Force to escape the Army draft. Another good friend of ours, Jimmy Barnes, was scheduled to join them, but J. C. said Jimmy backed out. Jimmy later confided in me that he was on the way to join up with his friends when lo and behold an attractive young lady made him a better offer, which he accepted. He was later drafted into the Army.

Following basic training, I was assigned permanent duty at Davis Monthan Air Force Base in Tucson, Arizona. My duty assignment at Tucson was as an administrative specialist assigned to the personal affairs office. I was assigned the job of managing the base Air Force Aid Society, and it was quite interesting. The job included a myriad of other duties in addition to those related to the Air Force Aid Society.

My primary job assignment introduced me to basic accounting challenges, which I had considered as a pursuit in college. I quickly discovered that this type of work was not something in which I would be interested in the future. I realized that I did not have the necessary patience for work like accounting. But not to worry, a new assignment was looming in my very near future.

I had been in my assignment for a little over one year. During that time I was dropped by my college sweetheart, and shortly afterward had married Gail Virginia Boyd of Tucson. We had established a home in a comfortable one-bedroom apartment and everything seemed to be going our way.

Unexpectedly, I received an order from base command to proceed to the Air Police office. When I asked the purpose, I was instructed to review an application for Washington, D. C., something to do with a Special Forces assignment. One candidate from our base was to be submitted for consideration. I objected to this, however, my name was submitted and a couple months later I was informed that I had been selected to serve in a top-secret special weapons squadron. I was ordered to report to Sacramento, California, as my base of operations. However, in the interim I was deployed for temporary duty at Francis E. Warren Air Force Base in Cheyenne, Wyoming. The purpose at Francis E. Warren was to receive cross training in supply services.

Upon my arrival at Cheyenne I again crossed paths with J. C. Shepherd. This time there was a new twist. Since we had left basic training, J. C. had married Mary Ruth Barnes of Berry. She was a cousin of Jimmy Barnes. They invited me over to their little apartment for dinner, and we had a very enjoyable evening talking about old times back in Berry. Having friends to visit with so far from home was really a boost to my morale.

I completed my training at Francis E. Warren by finishing assignment number one in my class and then proceeded to McClellan Air Force Base in Sacramento, California, where permanent party status would be determined later. All went well at McClellan. I applied myself and was selected to remain permanently at Sacramento. I think the primary reason that I was selected was the fact that I was the first to receive my top-secret security clearance. I immediately was assigned duties processing top-secret documents.

The assignment in California and my performance opened a door to my next assignment, which was as an administrative inspector for our field offices. One of the most pleasant field trips was a trip to Hickam Air Force Base in Honolulu, Hawaii, in 1956. I had the opportunity to visit the many monuments related to the World War II Japanese attack on Pearl Harbor, including the USS Arizona and other historic sites. Honolulu in 1956 was just a small, laid back town, and in the evenings the locals would gather on the beach and have an impromptu party.

Before that plush assignment, I was assigned to administrative duties for atomic bomb tests to be conducted at Mercury, Nevada, in February 1955. That assignment is covered elsewhere in this book. After completing four years in the Air Force, I was released from active duty on February 4, 1957. I remained in the inactive reserves for another four years before receiving an honorable discharge.

The four years in the Air Force taught me a great deal. I had the opportunity to truly grow up while working in a wide range of assignments with a variety of people. I also had a chance to experience over a dozen atomic bombs, an experience I will never forget. I sincerely hope no one ever has to experience that again. I also had the chance to develop managerial skills and to realize that I can produce at a higher level than most others. Each experience in life teaches us a valuable lesson. Some of them we may not want to learn, but they are all important in our development.

Atomic Bomb Tests

I have shared many of my life experiences. Now allow me to share one that was protected and hidden in secrecy for many years: my atomic bomb encounters.

I spent four years in the U. S. Air Force, and four months of that time was spent in Nevada's wasteland area of Mercury Base, located about 60 miles north of Las Vegas. The area was better known as Frenchman Flat or Yucca Flats, two dry lakebeds in the area.

My mission was to support the efforts of the 1009 Special Weapons Group participating in the spring of 1955 Teapot atomic bomb tests. I was 22 years old and never witnessed an atomic bomb detonation. I had viewed movie clips and news reports of the final days of World War II when atomic bombs were dropped on Hiroshima and Nagasaki, Japan, accelerating the surrender of Japan and bringing a swift end to the war.

I departed my home base in Sacramento, said goodbye to my wife, and set out on my trip to Nevada. I arrived on a cold afternoon in February 1955. As a matter of fact, snow covered the ground. My quarters were assigned, and when I located my quarters I discovered a plywood hut with no windows, only shutters that could be opened primarily for light and a breeze if desired. Inside was an oil-burning heater in the center of the one room. Unfortunately, the oil that normally fueled the heater was exhausted. The hut was equipped with eight bunks, each with a thin mattress. A single incandescent light bulb hanging from an exposed beam provided the only light. The quarters would sleep eight men, but when I arrived only one other occupant had checked in. Since we had no heat, we proceeded to the Quonset hut movie theater, not necessarily to enjoy the movie but to keep warm. Later that evening we received some oil for our heater and that provided some degree of heat—very little, but some.

On day two at Mercury I met the team I would be working with. Heading our team was Colonel Hendrix. Second in command was Major Nash from headquarters, Washington, D.C. There was also a captain and later a staff sergeant who was deployed to assist me with administrative duties. There were technical specialists deployed from our base in Sacramento. However, they were housed in barracks at Indian Springs Air Force Base a few miles south of us. One—Lou Watts—became a good friend of mine for many years. There were several others whose names I can't recall after so many years.

Lou and I talked about the tests of 1955 many times over the years. We often wondered what happened to the other people who participated in the tests. I recall that some of them also participated in the 1956 spring tests in the Atolls in the South Pacific. Several of those were exposed to such degrees of radiation that their lives were significantly shortened. The same might well have been true for many of the people who participated in the tests with us, but I lost track and was unable to communicate with them in the following years.

The runways for the aircraft participating in the tests were at Indian Springs Air Force Base. There were three particular aircraft that I recall very vividly. They were drone fighter jets that flew through one of the atomic bomb blasts at various altitudes to determine the effect that the bomb would have on aircraft flying in and near the test. The aircraft that was directed through the explosion at the lower altitude completely disintegrated. The bottom of the aircraft flying at the next higher was melted so badly that the landing gears would not come down. The third aircraft, flying even higher, seemed unaffected by the blasts.

Naturally, the first aircraft was no longer in existence. The second aircraft was so severely burned underneath and melted that it had to be destroyed in the mountains of the wastelands of Nevada. The third aircraft returned to its base normally, but as its wheels touched the aircraft lifted off the runway, then slammed into the ground and skidded off the end the runway.

That brought a lot of conjecture because it was required that personnel spray that aircraft down to eliminate most of the radiation. The people who were doing that kind of work at Indian Springs were very reluctant to go out and work on the aircraft since it was hot with radiation from the atomic bomb. Many days and weeks passed as the crippled aircraft sat as a monument just off the end of the runway. That "monument" was an on-going topic of conversation.

I had an opportunity to participate in more than a dozen—14 to be exact—atomic bomb blasts above ground. I witnessed each and every one from the vantage point of a command post that overlooked the dry lakebed at Yucca Flats, about one to two miles from ground zero. The bombs were devastating, and even to a 22-year-old airman it was a revelation that few would want to witness. I certainly hope that as a nation we never have the misfortune to experience something like that on our home soil.

One of my duties was to escort dignitaries from our office out to the command post location. When we arrived at the site, orders from the commander said that it if you had 4.5 density goggles you could observe the bomb straightaway. If you did not have these goggles you had to turn away from the blast, cover your eyes with both arms, and wait until an all clear was given. I was fortunate enough to have 4.5 density goggles. To better explain what 4.5 density means in layman's terms, if you wore a welding hood you could look at the sun and probably be able to see the sun clearly. With 4.5 density goggles, however, if you looked at the sun you could barely see the sun piercing through these very dark, dense goggles.

When the bombs were detonated, usually atop a 500-foot tower, and in one case dropped from an airplane on a parachute, the illumination from the bombs was so great that it would light up the inside of those 4.5 density goggles. It was horrific and frightening, to say the least, but what an experience it was! I still vividly remember the shock wave generated from each blast as it came across the desert floor.

It reminded me of the midsummer days back home in Berry when we kids would stand on the road or on the hot rails of the railroad track and see the tremendous heat waves wiggle across the road or down the railroad track. That particular site was personified greatly when those bombs exploded. The heat wave that came across in the shock wave was so intense that you could follow it from the bomb itself. Its approach was eerie, but more than that it penetrated one's body from front to back. It was something I had never felt before.

I have often shared with people my feelings by saying that witnessing one atomic bomb is adequate, but 14 was more than adequate. I spent four months at Mercury and observed each and every one. The thing that bothered me most about the tests of 1955 was the possible devastation the radiation fallout from the bombs might be causing people in the neighboring states of Utah and Montana. I questioned the authorities about the fallout and was told that we could let it go to the west for reasons of security at that time and that going to the east it really wouldn't bother anybody that much. But I noticed when the bombs were set off and the cloud drifted back toward our command post everyone scattered to get out of the way of the radiation, and justifiably so. Years later, we learned that we had done a great injustice to the people in Utah, Nevada and other areas from the radiation fallout.

Three of the 14 atomic bombs detonated at the Nevada test site in 1955 were more powerful than the 20-kiloton bomb dropped on Hiroshima, Japan, on August 5, 1945. That bomb killed an estimated 100,000 people. The largest Nevada bomb tested was 43 kilotons while others were 29 and 23 kilotons. My concern then and now is if we spread such harmful contamination over Japan in 1945, just how serious was our project in Nevada in 1955?

Years after my experience in Nevada I wondered why I only had one film badge that calculated the amount of radiation that one had on an outing. One film badge in four months, and I was there every day of the four months. I was aware that radiation had a half-life and so every time a bomb was exploded it added that degree of radiation to the ground in the surrounding area. I wondered what would happen to an individual who might have absorbed radiation in excess of the limits that were allowed. When I asked the limits that were allowed, either that was something not readily available or people just weren't concerned about it. We did get to go home once or twice on the weekends during our four months at Mercury. We were flown back to Sacramento on a DC-3 on Friday or Saturday, and I visited with my wife for one or two days before heading back to the desolate area of Mercury, Nevada, on Sunday.

I can't say that duty at the atomic tests site was an enjoyable time, but it was another learning experience. I spent many, many hours as administrative support working with our technicians in the field, helping them locate the remote testing sites that required startup, sometimes late at night. The tests would be called on or off depending on weather forecast.

Weather forecasting back in the 1950s was nothing like it is today. There were no computers and other advanced technology that we have in the 21st century. Instead, weather balloons were sent up to test the air movement at different altitudes because it was critical that we had a west to east breeze at critical altitudes to move the radiation cloud in the direction that was desired.

It was not uncommon for the test to be delayed due to undesirable wind aloft, and it was not unusual to have a test called back on at 10 at night. The late hour of the call did not permit helicopters to be deployed in pitch darkness to our remote seismology testing areas, so we had to use Jeeps to find the test facilities and prepare them for pre-dawn tests the next day. I have had many people ask me over the years about what happened in Nevada in 1955. For the longest time, I would not mention anything about what happened, what I had seen, or what I had experienced. After the declassification of the test sites and the fact that now you can read about it on the Internet I found it important to talk about those times.

A number of years after my military discharge I discovered in 1992 that I had developed prostate cancer requiring radical surgery. This was only six months after undergoing heart bypass surgery. Having two such serious conditions manifest themselves in such a short period of time brought back many questions relative to my exposure to excessive radiation during the Teapot Atomic Tests of 1955.

I approached the Veterans Administration to inquire about health problems related to the 1955 test in Nevada, but the process has been long and drawn out and is still unresolved. I have asked the VA to review my case over and over, and the only response I have received is that there is a backlog and they are still reviewing my case. It certainly seems to me that they are dragging their feet in an attempt to outlive me. Meanwhile, I cannot be admitted to a VA hospital or receive veterans benefits because my income is a little too great. That does seem to be a little ironic since in 1953 they accepted me in the Air Force with the understanding that if I fulfilled my duties of four years my country would fulfill its duties in making sure that I was taken care of. I did fulfill my commitment, however I feel neither the Air Force nor our government has upheld their contractual agreement.

Would I do it again? Would I go back through all of those high-risk assignments I experienced in Nevada? I wouldn't want to, but I won't say that I wouldn't do it. I did learn a lot from my experiences in the atomic tests of 1955.

I discovered that life offers many options and that there are multiple decisions we must address daily. Each opportunity nurtures growth. Each day of our lives there are decisions and crossroads. If we are to grow and develop and broaden our horizons we must take risks. There is a lot that can be accomplished. I took my job seriously, and I performed my duties in an exemplary manner. I received accolades from my commanding officer at the test site, and I received commendations from my base commander in Sacramento. But more than anything else, in my own heart I felt confident that I had done an exceptional job in the performance of my duties at Mercury, Nevada. In the end, I am glad that I performed my duties in the way that I did. I can hold my head high and be proud of my contributions.

There were so many little nuances that I uncovered about my life in the period of four months in Nevada. I had to test my endurance, my fortitude, my patience, and my ability to handle those types of hardships. Those hardships included being away from my family and friends, being separated from those I loved, and being placed in a situation in which I was uncomfortable and unsure of what the final outcome would be. I realized I was in the service of my country and my desire was to excel in the performance of my duties.

Today, the atomic bomb test site is closed and abandoned. There is no rumbling of atomic bombs on that desert floor. Nevada testing is simply a memory in my mind. My genuine desire and hope is that we will never see an atomic bomb or hydrogen bomb unleashed on our great nation, and I would certainly hope that we never find it necessary to drop such a bomb on any other country in the world.

Roy Dobbs
(U.S. Air Force)
(1953–1957)

The Struggles of Life

This portion of my book covers a number of years and multiple events. I will start with my first marriage, which was to Gail Boyd and lasted 18 years. Three wonderful children were the result of this marriage. Why it ended is difficult to say. I think it was because we had different expectations of life and different ideas on how to deal with the issues we faced. There were a number of crossroads and mountains to climb in our marriage. I would say that most of the problems or errors in judgment and decision-making were probably mine.

I met Gail while attending Emanuel Baptist Church in Tucson, Arizona, where I was stationed at Davis Monthan Air Force Base, and we quickly became a couple. Gail's mother was a delightful person to be around. She always prepared a fantastic Sunday dinner, which I enjoyed very much. I had my first exposure there to leg of lamb with some tasty green jelly sauce. It was a welcome departure from mess hall cooking at the base.

If the truth was known, I was probably looking for a home away from home. Gail's younger sister Nancy Jo was a pleasant person to be around, always smiling and laughing, and had a great pleasant attitude. Gail's dad was a supervisor with Mountain States Telephone Company in Tucson. He was what I would call straight laced and was definitely the man of the house. Mr. Boyd plotted the course, and the family marched to his drumbeat.

Gail was dating a young man in Tucson she had known since high school, but I snatched her away from him. I later wondered if I really should have prevailed. Maybe her old boyfriend was a better fit. Who knows? My personality and Gail's were very different. She questioned my motivations of pursuing a particular objective many times. She seemed always to compare my decisions to what her dad would have done in similar situations.

Gail and I were married in Tucson on June 3, 1954. I was a long way from home and all alone. To add insult to injury, I had received a "Dear John" letter from my fiancée Elizabeth back home in Alabama. She told me in the letter that she had changed her mind about our upcoming marriage. That experience dealt me a crushing blow, but I think my ego was damaged more than my heart. I had a history of rebounding quickly, however, and in this case I did just that and quickly fell in love with Gail.

Our marriage was successful in that it did yield three wonderful children. Virginia, our first child, was born November 30, 1955, and quickly became "Ginny." She was born in Sacramento, California, while I was stationed at

McClellan Air Force Base. Our second child, Roy David, was born three years later on August 8, 1958, in Phoenix, Arizona. Joseph Boyd, our third child, was born June 13, 1961, which happened to be Gail's birthday. They were all a blessing from God.

Gail and I rented a lovely one-bedroom apartment when we were first married and lived there for about a year. Gail had a job with the telephone company in Tucson and everything was going well. My mother was our most frequent visitor. She made a minimum of two trips per year while we were in Arizona and California. One day in 1954, I received orders to relocate to McClellan. After arriving in Sacramento I located living quarters for us on the ground floor of a large white frame home that had been converted into apartments. It was not fancy but it was adequate.

We later moved to a newly constructed apartment complex in Sacramento where many other military people lived. I met a young airman at McClellan named Gordon Sibbald. He was a California native and his mother lived along the coast at Capitols, California. Gordon and I became good friends right away and that friendship endured for a lifetime. Unfortunately, Gordon passed away in 2011. He and his wife Mary Ann were very close to Gail and me. I recall that on weekends we would cook a steak on the grill and then retire to the Sibbalds' living room. They had purchased a used seven-inch black-and-white television, and we would bunch up close to the TV and watch the Jackie Gleason show, "The Honeymooners."

In those days we could not afford luxury weekend trips, so we went camping instead. One of our favorite places to camp was Payson, Arizona, where we discovered some fine trout fishing. On one occasion, I recall that we traveled to the Sierra Mountains to a small motel and enjoyed a weekend of trout fishing on the Truckee River.

Gordon was a draftsman in the Air Force and his duties were different from mine. We were located in the same building and spent a lot of time together. Gordon and I usually brought a sandwich for lunch because there was not an appropriate dining facility in our building. We were both married and living off base, so mess facilities wasn't an option. Gordon and I would get together and talk about the upcoming weekends.

One day during our lunch hour, I saw Gordon eating a rather strange looking sandwich: two thin slices of white bread with something black in the middle. I asked what he was eating and Gordon said, "Haven't you ever heard of or eaten a black olive sandwich?" I replied that this was the first I had ever heard about such a sandwich. He immediately shared half of the sandwich with me and from that time forward I was hooked on black olives—not necessarily sandwiches mind you, but I can consume a large amount of whole black olives.

My four-year Air Force enlistment came to an end on February 3, 1957. Gail and I said our goodbyes to our friends and loaded Ginny in our vehicle and headed east and south. We made a stop in Phoenix for a brief visit with Gail's parents, who were living there then. Mr. Boyd had received a promotion and moved the 125 miles north. After a few days we turned our 1955 Pontiac east and headed for Alabama, where we spent a couple weeks with my mother and dad before returning to Phoenix.

During my tenure in the Air Force I operated the photography lab at the Airman's Club at McClellan Air Force Base. Prior to my departure from military service, I sought admission to Brooks Institute Photography, Santa Barbara, California. I received my admission papers just prior to my discharge from the Air Force.

Photography had been a dream since high school and now I was faced with a decision to pursue photography or abandon my dream. I had to consider the fact that I had a wife and daughter to support. I felt I should opt for a legitimate job, and I chose the telephone company. We all have difficult decisions to make, and I never looked back, only forward, as my mother had taught me. I felt that was the best decision for my family at the time, and I know now that it was. That was one of my early critical decisions. I was a married man with a beautiful new baby girl. I chose the safe way out and sought employment with Mountain States Telephone Company in Phoenix, Arizona.

In the back of my mind I continued to question my decision to pass up the Brooks Institute of Photography. Photography probably should have been my vocation based solely on my enjoyment and interest in the process. I have for many years been intrigued with photography. My brother Joe was first interested in photography, or at least he thought for a while that he was. He got a basic home darkroom setup for Christmas in 1947, but quickly lost interest and passed the simple equipment on to me. I became engrossed in both the picture taking and development process. I later purchased a small enlarger and that was the beginning of a lifetime love affair.

I had a successful career with the communications industry, but I always wondered what the outcome might have been if I had pursued my dream of photography. I have never lost my zeal for photography. I still enjoy capturing images on film and digital format. I often wish I had pursued photography as a career, but I am certain that I made the proper decision at that time, and photography has given me a life-long hobby.

On our return west, we bought a three-bedroom, two-bath home in north Phoenix that was still under construction and lived with Gail's parents until it was completed. The house did not have central air-conditioning, but it did have a swamp cooler that worked most of the time. The humidity in Phoenix was usually below five percent, so this type of cooling was adequate. The total price of the house was $10,850.

Gail's father was instrumental in helping me get an interview with Mountain States Telephone Company. I passed all the interviews and medical exam and expressed a desire to join the marketing department; however, the only position open was as a central office frame man. I needed a job and felt I could eventually work my way into the marketing department. I started out in the downtown central office and within a few months was able to transfer to the North Phoenix office, which was closer to our residence.

My next assignment was in the outside maintenance department as a cable repairman, where I spent six months before receiving a call for an interview in marketing. I made the grade and was given the position, which soon led to the position of sales engineer.

Keep in mind that in 1957 I was a new employee with the telephone phone company and my pay was $200 a month. Our house payment was $78, and that was pretty steep at my income level. I will offer some comparisons to what things cost back in those days. Blue Cross Blue Shield insurance was $6.50 a month for our family, sirloin steak was 79 cents a pound, and gasoline was 30 cents a gallon. Quite a difference from today, isn't it? However, when I was a boy in Berry gasoline was only 17 cents a gallon. From 1929 until 1974 gas remained under 50 cents a gallon. That's not the case today, of course. Everything has changed, and our lives have changed along with the times. Things change and we must accommodate change whenever it occurs.

Gail and I had moved to a new city and a new neighborhood where we didn't have a single friend. That changed very soon, however. We spotted a young couple looking at the home just behind ours and introduced ourselves, and a long-term friendship was born. They were Harold (Bud) and Lindel Fields, and were expecting their first child. They were pretty much in the same boat as we were, with low-paying jobs at a local bank. However, they both were employed. Bud shared with me later that he was not even sure their combined wages would allow them to qualify for a FHA loan with payments of about $90 per month. With a child on the way, he expressed grave concerns about the payments. They made it, however, and had three children (Randy, Ronnie and Rachel) during the eight years we were their neighbors. They all still live in the Phoenix area, and Bud and Lindel and I have remained close friends to this day.

Gail and I had our second child, a son, in 1958. We decided to give him my name of Roy, but not junior; we chose David. My mother always called him Roy David, and she called my daughter Ginny Gwen. We were now a family of four, and I realized that I needed to generate more income to support my growing family. I worked 8 to 5 at the telephone company, which left the evenings and weekends open for a second job. I landed a job at the local drive-in theater. I didn't get dark until about 8, so I had time to come home and have dinner with the family before going to my second job.

I quickly became assistant manager of the theater, and the pay and working conditions greatly improved. I hired a friend of mine from the telephone company, Albert Taylor, who worked the lot checking the trunks of the cars and under the blanket in the back seat for teenagers trying to sneak into the drive-in without paying. Such stunts were pretty prevalent back in those days. The movies would generally go beyond midnight, and I would hurry home to get five or six hours sleep before facing the same routine again the next day. That routine was pretty much a seven-day-a-week job.

In the 1950s, this was often the routine for a young man struggling to provide for his family. I later received several promotions at the phone company and was compensated adequately, allowing me to give up my second job.

I began classes at Phoenix Junior College on the G.I. Bill in 1958 and earned an associate degree in Arts and Sciences. Later I entered Grand Canyon College, a Baptist supported school. I continued my formal education along with voice lessons. I enjoyed singing under the direction of a Doctor Bagg. He was an outstanding voice teacher, and I enjoyed my association with him. I was approaching my senior year at Grand Canyon in 1964 when I decided I wanted to return home to Alabama.

In 1964, my brother Joe suddenly lost his first wife. She entered the hospital for what seemed to be a routine appendectomy, but something went wrong and she quit breathing. In those days, surgery was not like it is today. When the medical staff discovered she was not breathing it was too late. That was a devastating time for Joe, who was the father of three boys and a girl, and for all of us. I chose to fly home to be with my brother and to help in any way I could.

While in Alabama, I realize that I missed my home state a great deal. This was my home, and I had been away for too long. I decide to return to Alabama. I interviewed with the Southern Bell Telephone marketing department in Birmingham and received an immediate offer to relocate to Birmingham. I met with North Alabama Division Marketing Manager Ernest Herlong. I had not yet discussed this proposal for change with my wife, my children, or my employer in Phoenix. Mr. Herlong said, "I want you back here, and I will make all the necessary arrangements to get you transferred to Southern Bell Telephone Company."

I returned to Phoenix to break the news to my family and share my intentions with my management at Mountain States Telephone Company. I was never sure my wife bought into this move. My employer in Phoenix wished me well, and I sold our home and loaded up a U-Haul truck and headed for my new assignment in Montgomery, Alabama. I had already understood that the assignment would not be in Birmingham, but in Montgomery, Alabama, as the account manager for state government.

I had made arrangements for Gail, Ginny, David and Joe to return to Birmingham by train. My parents met them in Birmingham and provided the comforts for them there until I arrived in Montgomery. The trip from Phoenix to Montgomery was, to say the least, a hair-raising and dangerous trip. The 1750-mile trek from Phoenix to Montgomery on narrow roads was difficult, and at times I had trouble locating service stations I could access because I was also towing a totally overloaded Chevrolet station wagon. It may sound simple but it wasn't. The tow bar I rented from U-Haul was comparable to wiring a flimsy piece of metal to the bumper of the old Chevrolet and hoping and praying it might make it. I replaced the tow bar a couple of times when I could find a location that had a U-Haul dealership.

With very little sleep coupled with three days of tough driving, I made it to Cuba, Alabama, before the tow bar again gave out in an area where there was no U-Haul dealer to help me. I finally managed to locate an elderly gentleman who did welding, and he patched the tow bar up for the final leg to Montgomery. My new boss, Frank Robison, and his wife Betty met me on Highway 80 just west of Montgomery and directed me on into Montgomery, where Gail and the children and Mother and Dad were anxiously awaiting my arrival at the Holiday Inn. Betty Robison was a realtor, and she had located us a nice home on Sir Michael Drive in Montgomery at a cost of $26,000—almost three times the cost of our home in Arizona. We moved in, and I began my work assignment as the state government account manager immediately.

Over the next 14 years, the move from Phoenix to Montgomery produced many significant milestones in my life. I worked closely with both Governor George Wallace and his wife, Governor Lurleen Wallace. In 1972 I completed my bachelor's degree from Auburn University, and I became deeply involved in civic work in Montgomery with the Jaycees and the Optimist clubs.

Gail and I were divorced in 1972, and she quickly moved the family back to Phoenix, Arizona. I don't believe Gail ever really enjoyed Alabama; it was too far from her parents and her comfort zone. She seemed unable to accept my desire to reach my full potential, and she found fault in the fact that I often did not do things as her father would have. She felt that our three children were the only concern. I shared with her that we had both vowed to love and care for each other. I think she felt that obligation had been fulfilled and at 40 years old I was selfish if I harbored any other desires. When I presented my case, she accused me of being a selfish person.

To this day, I believe Gail really required the security of her father and mother and that she moved back to Phoenix mainly for that reason. As she left, she expressed concerns that I would grow old as a sad and lonely man. To the contrary, I have spent the last 40 years enjoying the love and admiration of a caring and sharing wife. My one regret is that Gail never had the opportunity to enjoy a full life with a mate. Gail passed away in 2012 as a result of a rare brain tumor.

Years with Governor Wallace

I first met Alabama Governor George C. Wallace in 1965. I had just returned to Alabama from Arizona and was working with Southern Bell Telephone Company as the state government account manager in Montgomery. Our first meeting was very professional, pleasant and cordial. I explained to him that my job was representing the telephone industry to the state of Alabama and that my intent was to provide the very best telecommunication services available to state government on a statewide basis.

I spent most of the time from 1965–1967 learning exactly what the state's telecommunications needs were and how Southern Bell could play a part in improving those services. I had very little contact with Wallace, primarily due to the time I was spending with department heads and different areas of state government.

In November 1967, as Wallace was preparing to open his 1968 presidential campaign headquarters in Montgomery, I, along with some other officials from Southern Bell, met with Wallace and his staff at the Wallace for President Headquarters. In those days, the telephone industry made one person available to assist serious presidential candidates with their telecommunication services nationwide, and I was chosen to be that representative with the Wallace campaign. I was given the option of either taking a leave of absence from the telephone company and going as a member of Wallace's campaign staff or remaining with the telephone company. I choose to remain on the Southern Bell payroll, representing the telephone industry.

My first assignment was to set up a telecommunications network in the headquarters offices for the Wallace campaign in Los Angeles, California, where he was seeking recognition as an independent on the ballot in the Democratic Primary in California. Upon arrival in California, I met Bob Cheney, a representative from Pacific Bell. Bob was so helpful. He was quick to provide everything we needed or asked for. Bob was obviously interested in providing good telecommunication services for Wallace's campaign. I met Bob's wife, Hetty, and his son, mother and father. His son is now a senior pilot with American Airlines. My, how time flies!

The effort to get on the California ballot was not a simple one for Wallace. It seemed as though the registrar's office and whoever was in charge made it very difficult for anyone to change parties to get in the Independent Party to register as a delegate for Wallace. However, that was finally successfully accomplished.

We continued to develop offices throughout California for people to work for the Wallace campaign. After that was done, I returned to Montgomery and met with Governor Wallace and his staff. They expressed their pleasure with my work in California and asked me to serve as the Wallace representative for all their telecommunications needs and be responsible for all offices throughout the United States. I was given responsibility for all the news media, the Secret Service, and our local State Troopers' telecommunications needs.

Those early years of travel were very interesting. We traveled in everything from a two-engine Cessna aircraft to the DC-6B and DC-7, both four-engine aircraft, and finally two four-engine electors. They were very noisy and lacked most comforts compared to today's air travel. We had some great times. Our pilots were state employees and were extremely proficient. I had the chance to sit in the cockpit with them many times, talk with them, and observe their techniques of flying. They were excellent pilots.

Later on in 1968 the Wallace campaign really started picking up steam and there were whistle stops every day. I traveled with Wallace seven days a week, and we were out in different locations every day, sometimes even making two and three different states in a single day. Many times traveling was difficult because we didn't have jet aircraft—just prop-engine aircraft.

We spent many hours in the air. Governor Wallace would give interviews to various members of the press as we made our way to our next destination, where we were met by a number of local media and supporters. I had installed telephone and teletype communications systems aboard the aircraft for use by the media, of course.

One of our more memorable stops was at a small airport in Roanoke, Virginia. When the aircraft came to rest the local telephone representative came up and said, "Well, we got everything installed." I said, "We don't have the lines inside the airplane," and he said, "Well, that's all I'm going to do. That's all the orders I have." I suggested to him that he call his district supervisor. He said he was not calling anyone, particularly not at his district level, because he had his orders, and he suggested that I call them. I called them, and when the district boss arrived the activity became fierce. The boss proceeded to make the necessary connections, and the young installer got a strong reprimand that he will probably long remember. There were things that had to be done right away, and we didn't have time to discuss or quibble over them.

I recall seeing Wallace seated on the aircraft once when the noise level was very high. He was having a conversation with a member of the media while also browsing through the Wall Street Journal. At the same time, he was attuned to other conversations going on in the aircraft and would quickly correct any individual who was giving out erroneous information. I later said to Governor Wallace, "I know you have some hearing aids and that you claim to be hard of hearing, but at times it seems to me that there may be selective hearing. There are things that you want to hear and other things that you don't want to hear." He just smiled and said, "Well, Roy, it works pretty well."

There was one instance early in the 1968 campaign that I fondly recall. The campaign was in Providence, Rhode Island, and Governor Wallace invited me to ride with him to the auditorium where he was speaking that evening. I graciously agreed, and on the way there we talked and had an enjoyable conversation. As we arrived at the auditorium where the governor was to speak, there were a number of protesters there carrying signs and making terrible threats and comments. As we exited the car, there was some pushing, swinging and hitting. It was dangerous for a while.

I commented to Governor Wallace, "You signed on for this presidential run; I didn't. I

signed on to take care of your telecommunications needs and I will do that. I will do
whatever is needed; you don't have to worry
about that. But if you need me you can locate
me behind the press, and I will ride on the bus
with the press because no one bothers the
press."

I found that to be a very valuable
experience with Governor Wallace, and as I
shared with many people, I felt that there was
going to be a time when it would not be rocks,
fists and vile words but also the possibility
bullets flying, and I did not want to be in the
line of fire. So from that time on I stood behind
the CBS news film crew, which included
Laurens Pierce, his soundman, and the light
man. I even commented to Laurens once, "If
anything ever does happen to Governor
Wallace, I'm sure you will be in the forefront."
He was always there.

In 1976 Wallace was campaigning in
Maryland, and I was back in Alabama preparing
to go to Miami, Florida, to set up telephone
services for his campaign headquarters at the
National Democratic Convention. Laurens
Pierce and his CBS camera crew were in the
front when Wallace was shot. Laurens received
the Pulitzer Prize for filming of the attempted
assassination of Wallace.

Many people have asked me why they
never saw me on television during Wallace's

campaign. Everybody seemed to crowd around Wallace hoping to get on the daily news, but I simply felt that somewhere along the line something was going to happen to Governor Wallace, and I did not want to be a part of that. I just did my job and that's all I wanted to do. As the years progressed, however, and the campaigns were behind us, Wallace was making headway in the 1970s and particularly in the last campaign he ran before the attempted assassination. He had really gained momentum, and many of us felt that he would be the candidate on the Democratic ticket for that year. Unfortunately, the attempt on his life spoiled his aspirations for president. That event might have derailed his campaign for president, but it didn't mitigate or minimize his zeal for politics.

Governor Wallace was one of the most outstanding politicians I ever met in my life. I had the opportunity to meet Richard Nixon, Hubert Humphrey, Lyndon B. Johnson, and several others, but George Wallace, in my opinion, was the epitome of a politician. He could read and motivate an audience like no one else. Over the years, my relationship with Governor Wallace grew deeper and deeper. We had a mutual respect for each other.

I vividly remember another occasion where Governor Wallace expressed deep confidence in my performance. We were in a staff meeting and an individual questioned my sincerity and my commitment to the campaign. The room was filled with some 45 or 50 top-level political analysts and Wallace's top advisors. The comment was made that I was arranging all the telecommunications and my work should be checked by someone else before they paid the bills.

Governor Wallace looked around very candidly in his own inimitable way and said, "There is only one person in this room that I trust implicitly." He paused for a few seconds, and the room became deadly quiet. You literally could have heard a pin drop. He said, "That person is Roy Dobbs, and if he puts his initials on anything on my behalf I do not want anyone to ever question it. Is that understood?" There was a long pause of silence before his campaign director said, "Yes, sir. We all understand." Wallace said, "What's next?" and the meeting continued. That was how he did business.

Governor Wallace and I were more than acquaintances; we were friends, and we remained life-long friends. I always enjoyed being around him and Mrs. Wallace and their family. At times I felt like a family member myself.

Mrs. Wallace's election as governor of the state of Alabama was a historic time for our state. Some people might claim that Mrs. Wallace did not have the credentials to serve as governor of Alabama. I was around Mrs.

Wallace in the Governor's Mansion and at her home where she served as a wife and mother. She enjoyed life. She was a well-rounded individual, and Mrs. Wallace was not only elected governor, she served as governor.

One of my favorite stories about Mrs. Wallace occurred during her early days in office. She called me one morning and said, "Roy, would you come to my office? There is something I want you to do." When I arrived at her office, I inquired as to the specifics of my assignment. With just the two of us in the office, she said, "I would like for you to arrange a buzzer on George's (her husband, the former governor and her number one aide and advisor) desk in Room 101 across the hall." I said, "Do you mean, Governor, that you want me to put an intercom between your phone and Governor George?" She said, "No, not at all. I want you to put a buzzer on his desk and a push button here on my desk so that whenever I push the button, it will buzz George's desk, and when I buzz him I want him to hop up and get over here to address things that I need ask to him."

I asked Governor Lurleen Wallace if I could have the privilege of sharing her demands with Governor George Wallace. She laughed and said, "Sure, go on over and share it with George." Governor George was sitting at his desk working in a very meager office. I went in and said, "Governor George, Governor Lurleen wants me to put a button on her desk and a buzzer on your desk so that when she pushes that button and buzzes you she wants you to hop up and immediately get over there." Governor George looked at me and said, "Roy, she really means that, too."

There are many other stories I could share about my time with the Wallace family at the mansion. I spent many hours at the mansion with Governor George Wallace in particular. We talked about everything from politics to remote telephone conferences. Governor George was familiar with amplified telephone addresses, whether they were around the Montgomery area, around Alabama, or in another state. Governor Wallace always wanted me to go to that area and arrange the telecommunications for that remote telephone call. I represented the telephone industry, and I was always happy to do it.

I remember one evening when Governor George called and said, "Roy, I'm going to be speaking to the Farm Bureau of Florida in Gainesville and I'd like you to go down with Red Bamberg, director of the Alabama Development Office, and some other Wallace supporters." The governor wanted everything to be perfect and to make sure the conference call with Florida was handled properly. He also said, "Let me know what you think when you see the crowd. Assess the situation and advise me of the number of attendees and the general lay of the land." "I certainly will, Governor," I answered.

That evening, flying down on Governor Wallace's private plane, Red Bamberg opened a bottle of bourbon, and I suggested to him that he should be very careful because "as you know, Governor George does not drink and does not condone it, certainly not on his airplane." The bottle was eventually spilled on the carpet and knowing that the aroma stays for a long time, I didn't say anything. I felt sure that Governor George would detect the presence of alcohol. I set up the telecommunications as requested, and the governor he did a splendid job of speaking. He handled the situation with poise and enthusiasm, as always.

I was in Governor Wallace's private office in Montgomery the day that the assassination attempt was made on his life in Maryland. All of us were in shock as we heard the disturbing news over the intercom. We really did not know at that time whether he would live or die. Knowing Governor Wallace, I felt that if there were a chance of living, he would do so. He was a fighter, and his faith in God would surely help him make it.

After a lengthy stay in the hospital, Governor Wallace finally came home. Not long afterward, we were talking in his private office when he made a startling comment to me. He said that his life had been totally destroyed, that he felt so bad and everything was so difficult for him now. He said, "I really wish the assailant had taken my life instead of leaving me in this limited capacity. This is truly a fractured life."

Many of us encouraged Governor George to go on because he had so much to give, so much to offer other people. Over the next few years he and I enjoyed a richer friendship, one that really blossomed even more because whatever he asked me to do, I did. It mattered not if we were sitting in the mansion talking about things or whether we were in his private office. We had a very close relationship based on mutual respect. I have been asked why I have not written a book on George Wallace. My response is simply that there have been several books written about Governor Wallace and most are less than accurate. I just want to remember our lasting relationship.

The campaigns themselves held many mysteries. I recall Governor Wallace telling me about the campaign of 1964, a presidential run which he entered on a limited basis. He was in a close run in Maryland for the Democratic nomination for president. The 6 p.m. news regarding the Maryland election said Wallace was leading early on. He came back later and made the comment that after a thorough recapitulation, Wallace was now trailing in the election. Governor Wallace always said jokingly that he didn't understand what recapitulation meant, but if someone said they're going to recapitulate on you, you had better watch out; they're going to do something bad to you. He had a sense of humor.

In many press conferences and interviews on such television shows as "Meet the Press," "Issues and Answers" and "Face the Nation" on which he appeared, some members of the national news media tried to belittle Wallace because he was, in their opinion, a southern redneck and not worthy to be president of the United States. I have always wondered what makes those people such authorities.

But in my opinion, Governor Wallace was head and shoulders above most of the candidates he faced. I shall never forget one Sunday morning on ABC news Sam Donaldson was interviewing Governor Wallace and attempted to cut him off at every opportunity, refusing to permit Wallace to respond to any of the questions he asked. Finally Donaldson asked Wallace about his stand on busing little children from one school to another for effective integration. Governor Wallace simply said that he had nothing against busing if it were the will of the families to move their children from one point to another, but he just didn't like the idea of forcing someone to have to go long distances just to simply achieve a racial balance. Donaldson quickly cut him off and did not let the Governor complete his answer. Donaldson asked another question then paused and said, "Governor Wallace, are you going to answer that question?" Governor George calmly replied, "Mr. Donaldson, if you will be quiet long enough for me to answer, I'll answer any question that you have."

It would be very difficult to sit in a meeting like that with someone belittling you on every avenue every time, never giving you really any credit for anything, but George Wallace was a bigger man than any news person I ever talked with. He was head and shoulders above them all. He was a true gentleman. You might call him a Southern Gentleman. But he was more than that. He loved people. He demonstrated that by his compassion for people. There is story after story that I am personally familiar with where George Wallace showed his concern for other individuals and their families.

Governor George Wallace chaired the Southern Governors Conference at Point Clear in Mobile in 1973, and I was given the opportunity to arrange all the telecommunications services for the meeting. I did so and received a well done from Governor Wallace. The next year the Southern Governors Conference was held in Houston, Texas, sponsored by the governor of Texas, and I was asked by the state of Texas and Southwestern Bell to go to Houston to help them with the telecommunications arrangements there. That was a real honor for me. The officials realized that it was successful in Alabama, and they wanted to make it just as good or better in Texas.

A side story involving Governor George and me happened in 1979. I was finishing my year as district governor of Optimist International and we had our annual meeting in Montgomery. We had a big evening recognition banquet. I called Governor Wallace, who was out of office at that time, and asked him if he would be my guest at the Optimist International dinner, at which I was host, and he graciously accepted. We were all sharply dressed in tux and black tie. We sat and talked at the head table, and he turned to my wife Phyllis and said, "I want to thank you for sharing Roy with me over these great many years. He gave his time to my efforts and my family."

The final chapter to the George Wallace story came some years after his death. I talked to his surviving wife, Lisa Taylor Wallace, and Lisa shared with me some very, very heart-warming stories. Lisa says that she and Governor George would reminisce after he was out of office and that he often said, "I wonder why Roy Dobbs didn't visit us at the mansion." Lisa went on further to say that Governor George on many occasions had compared people as they just talked as husband and wife and that Governor George said of all the people he had ever known in his life—and that was many—he had "never met a person with the integrity of Roy Dobbs."

Words are not adequate to tell how that statement made me feel. Recognition, accolades and awards are one thing, but when you have someone of George Wallace's stature make that kind of statement about you, it means a lot. Governor Wallace said that during all the campaigns of 15 years that we were together, including three presidential campaigns, "I never had to check with Roy to see if the telecommunications services were there. Whatever we needed was always there. Roy always had them there before time, or at least on time, every time, and he said that kind of person was hard to find." That's what I take pride in: a job well done. By rising above mediocrity, I can perform my duties in a lot less strenuous way.

I could easily have performed my duties with far less effort and still gotten the job done and, no one would have known the difference except me. But the one person I wanted to satisfy more than anyone else was me, and when I did that I felt like my efforts were above and beyond what most other people could or would have done. I took pride in my performance in all the jobs I did. Yes, George Wallace taught me a lot. His administration taught me a lot, and the experience of three presidential campaigns with him served me well during my years as mayor of Berry.

I am grateful that I had an opportunity to know Governor George Wallace, and I say again that Governor Lurleen Wallace was truly an outstanding lady. She was a classy person. Certainly she fought uphill battles, too, but she did it with dignity. She was a fine governor and a wonderful friend, also.

Civic Involvement

I had never been involved in civic organizations until I moved to Montgomery in 1965. A friend in our neighborhood invited me to attend a meeting of the Capital City Jaycees, and I went with him. I was impressed with the organization and joined that evening. Within just a couple years I worked myself up to president of the organization and in that role assisted the club in pulling itself out of a financial deficit to become profitable.

One of the key things the club did was sponsor a local Miss Universe Alabama pageant. In about 1967 Sylvia Hitchcock won the contest in Montgomery and later won the Miss Universe world title. The dilemma was to get Sylvia back the next year at our local contest was expensive. The executive committee had big visions of staging a huge show the next year. I pointed out that we had lost about $2,500 the first year, and my question to the board members was, "Why would we want to get into a losing proposition?" One response was, "We can hire a headliner comedian, rent the Coliseum, and maybe the project would be profitable." The key word was maybe. I commented that maybe we need to look at it and determine if we can make it profitable. After a thorough review of the expenses and what it would cost to get Sylvia back to appear on stage, the best we could do would to be lose $4,000.

"Is this what you recommend? You want to lose $4,000?" I asked the young man on the executive committee. My argument was that since we had lost $2,500 the year before, we needed to get involved in something that would be profitable so that we can get the organization out of the red and back into the black again.

They all agreed, and our next adventure was to sponsor the state convention of the Alabama Jaycees, which we did. It turned out to be very profitable, and we were able to satisfy our bank notes and get back on our feet. The idea of this piece is to let people know that there are times you have to make difficult decisions based on facts and not fiction or wishful thinking. You have to exercise sound, rational judgment. That's what we did in that case, and it taught me a great deal about financial management and leadership skills. It also taught me that you sometimes have to make decisions that are not really popular.

Later on I graduated from the Jaycees, because the age limit was 35. My next challenge in Montgomery was to associate with the Downtown Optimist Club. Optimist International is an organization that works primarily with young people, promoting a myriad of programs that benefit youth and community. I became very active in that organization, serving as vice president and president. I had the opportunity as vice president to oversee our fund-raising project for that year, which was a barbecue chicken and camp stew sale. We sold all over the Montgomery area, and it was a very successful program.

The program had to be revived every year from scratch, with someone figuring out what, when, where, who and how we did it. I solved that problem by writing a program of policy on exactly where everything came from, where to start, what to do, who to contact (with telephone numbers), and that program became a written policy that was passed on to the incoming president. Each new president found it to be extremely helpful since he didn't have to reinvent the wheel every year. That was another lesson I carried with me to the next level.

The next level was my involvement in District Optimist International as the District Governor for Alabama and Mississippi. There I found myself involved in a situation where our district had been substandard for many years. We were content to be on the bottom, representing the bottom. I asked my lieutenant governors—there were 12 of them from the states of Mississippi and Alabama—to join together and work my plan that would move our district up from the bottom.

My plan was to elevate our district that was normally in number 39th place at the bottom to the number one position. My lieutenant governors, however, felt that I was demanding the impossible when I asked them to join me in the execution of the plan that I had developed. I promised them that if each and every one of us would work that plan for one year we could reach our goal of becoming number one internationally. There was some hesitation and there were some people who didn't feel it could work, but in the end we all signed on as a team to work together, and at the end of 1979 we were ranked first internationally. The pride exhibited by all our members was well worth the effort. They realized that we had accomplished something difficult that very few people had done. That accomplishment gave them a lot of pride and motivation.

We finished number two or number three the next year, but it's hard to stay on top. It is sometimes difficult to get to the top, but we did it. After serving as district governor for Alabama and Mississippi, Phyllis and I went on to serve in the international levels on the finance committee, the membership committee, chairman of the international convention committee, and later in 1982, as international vice president. All of the steps along the way helped me realize that being at the top is a lot better than being in the middle or being on the bottom, and the only way we get to the top is to establish lofty goals then push ourselves and make sure that we get there. In doing so, we take ourselves to the top, and many times we help others elevate themselves, also.

The one thing for which I received the most gratification is in knowing that we have helped others along the way to realize that you don't have to settle for mediocrity. As football coaches constantly tell their players, you can always do more and better than you think. The only requirement is a commitment: working together, working with people, and sharing the rewards.

Organizations like Optimist International, Jaycees, and other organizations I have been affiliated with helped hone my managerial skills while proving to be sound developmental tools. All were significant training grounds for me. In later years those experiences played an important part in the years that I served as mayor and in other jobs that I had. It was a great time, a lot of fun, and we did a lot of good for not only ourselves but many other people along the way.

A College Degree After All

During my 30-year tenure as a marketing manager with the Bell telephone companies, I spent a number of years in Montgomery. I had the opportunity to work with many fine people there, and one of those was Frank Robison, our district marketing manager.

Frank would always have a loaded agenda for meeting with marketing managers, and he was notorious for trying to use metaphors to illustrate a point. Many times they would be tremendously misdirected, mixed metaphors. We sat around delegating different managers the responsibility to capture the mixed metaphor. We would all pretend to be taking notes, not to give away the one actually capturing the "goodie." One guy writing all the time would have given us away or tipped our hand, so we all continued to write as though we were taking important notes.

I recall several times when Frank would get so excited telling a story that the words were quite difficult to follow. He said one day, "You know, it's almost like going up the wrong creek with a broken paddle." On another occasion, he said, "The horse is out of the gate and running down the path." My favorite one came when just he and I were in his office. He was so excited that he literally could not contain himself. The subject related only to me. I thought I understood what he was getting at, but he told me, "I have something I need to share with you, but I can't tell you." I said, "Well, Frank, if you can't tell me I can understand. Maybe it's something that is confidential and now is just not the appropriate time. It will just have to wait until a later time."

He said, "By, George, I'm going to tell you." I said, "Well, okay," and he said, "Well, there is some good stuff coming down for you, but I don't want you to count your chickens before they're signed." I had never heard "count your chickens before they're signed." I thought it was "count your chickens before they're hatched." The reference he was making was good news for me because it was a sizable increase in my pay, for which I was very grateful.

I maintain a list of Frank's mixed metaphors and retrieve them from time to time and enjoy a silent chuckle. He was a good man and a great friend. It serves to help recall many pleasant memories during my tenure with the telephone company in Montgomery.

There was another person who was very instrumental in my returning to college to complete my undergraduate degree. That person was Travis Shipp. Travis worked for me at the time, and he had a real desire to see people move ahead. Travis was aware that I only lacked a few hours to finish my undergraduate work, and he and I both were aware that Auburn University offered night classes in Montgomery.

I considered taking the necessary classes, but initially found a myriad of excuses not to do it. I was traveling with Governor Wallace as communications director for his political campaigns. I had the job of managing the state government account for Southern Bell Telephone Company. Add to that, I had a family, and I just didn't have the time. But thank God Travis was relentless and continued to work on me until I signed up for evening classes.

I attended class from 5:40 p.m. until 10 p.m. four nights a week, and it wasn't easy. I'd been out of school a long time and getting back in the routine of classroom work, homework and essay writing was really not my forte. Travis was right there to help and encourage me. He taught me a lot, and I hope that I was able to teach him something about marketing. Travis was only a few hours shy of having his PhD degree at the University of Georgia.

One day, Travis approached me with the question of whether he should go back to Georgia and finish his PhD or stay with the phone company, where he had a bright future also. "Travis, are you asking me a question, or you telling me what your desires really are?" I asked. "I feel you already know what you are going to do; you simply want my blessings and concurrence." I explained that I knew that his first love was in education, whatever he did.

Before coming to the phone company, Travis had been a captain in the Army Rangers. He was a straight shooter and he was good at whatever he choose to pursue. He returned to Georgia and finished his PhD. A couple of years ago I had a chance to talk with Travis and found out that he had retired from the University in Indiana. We had an opportunity to reminisce and talk about the old days and that was rewarding. The first thing he asked me was, "Do you still have that long list of mixed metaphors we compiled in Frank's staff meetings?" I assured him that I had the original hand-written copy. I thanked Travis again for his encouragement to continue my education at Auburn and to get my undergraduate degree.

I graduated in 1972, 20 years after I entered The University of Alabama in 1952. Some people inquired why I went back to college when I was already a marketing manager with the phone company. They felt I had nothing to gain by earning a college degree at that point in my life. I looked them squarely in the eyes and said, "It will do me a lot of good," and it did. Not only did I gain knowledge, I gained renewed confidence in my ability to accomplish whatever goals I set.

I earned my degree the hard way, too. I had a full-time job and pretty much traveled with Governor George Wallace during his presidential campaign. I had a heavy load at Auburn University at night and a family to which I gave a little bit of time. It was not an excessive price to pay, but it wasn't all that great. In retrospect, I'm extremely grateful that I did pursue my undergraduate degree.

I am proud of the accomplishment because it taught me that people could do pretty much what they want to do if they are willing to pay the price. Many people have asked me if I thought I could do everything. The answer to that is obviously no, but I do think I can do anything that I set my mind to do. There are many proud accomplishments in my life, and being an Auburn University graduate is one of them. As I recall my college career, I am reminded of the adage, "Difficult tasks can be accomplished right away; impossible tasks take a little longer."

My college degree helped prepare me for the job as mayor of Berry, something I never thought I would become. It also reminded me that one should never stop reaching for that higher rung on the ladder, to never stop dreaming, and to never stop growing. You should always continue to prepare for the unseen opportunities that lie ahead. I believe if you are prepared the opportunities will come. If you are not prepared, you cannot take advantage of those opportunities.

A New Beginning

    I met Phyllis Henson in 1972, and we were married on October 12, 1973. We have since enjoyed more than 40 years of happiness and several very successful undertakings during our years together. Phyllis was a sales representative for Southern Bell Telephone in Montgomery. She had transferred there from Cocoa Beach, Florida, in 1965 and initially worked in the business office. Phyllis and I met when she transferred to the marketing department and became a member of the state government account team.

    Phyllis has been the wind beneath my wings, and she considers me her soul mate. Our life together has been a whirlwind. With our marriage, Phyllis became the stepmother of our three wonderful children. We have since added 10 grandchildren and now have seven great grandchildren. David and his wife live near us on Pleasant Hill Farm. Joe, who attended the University of Arizona and the Southwest Baptist Theological Seminary before serving as pastor of a church in Arizona, is now involved in humanitarian work in Africa, where he lives with his wife and two children. Virginia has remained in Phoenix, where she and her husband have raised six children.

We moved from Montgomery to Birmingham in 1979, and Phyllis continued working in the marketing department. She traveled five states, while I traveled nine states at that time.

I retired from BellSouth Telephone Company in 1987 at age 54 after 30 years with the company, taking advantage of an attractive early retirement offer as the company downsized. I felt then that there was another challenge looming on the horizon, and I was eager to discover and pursue it. Phyllis had not yet completed her 20 years with the telephone company, so she continued to work as we explored our options, including a possible move back to Berry.

My mother, who was living with us in Birmingham, was excited when we suggested the possibility of reclaiming the old family farm on Pleasant Hill and making our home there. "Are you really considering going back to Berry?" my mother asked. "It's just a thought," I explained. "We all must agree that it is the best idea." Mother quickly gave her response. "I agree." Although moving to the small town of Berry was a new experience for Phyllis, she was game for whatever we decided upon. We all made the decision to move back to Berry. My mother was so excited that she exhibited characteristics of a giddy little girl. She was finally going home.

Phyllis and I had planned for our retirement. We had made sound investments to supplement our retirement income, and when we sold our home in Birmingham we had sufficient cash to build our home in Berry.

As we began the move, I spent several days a week in Berry preparing for our transition to country living. The first order of business was to build a two-and-a-half-acre lake on the property directly behind our selected home site. We desperately wanted a fishing place of our very own, and the lake was completed in 1988.

Phyllis, Mother and I, along with my son David and his wife, Karen, and their daughters Amanda and Sarah, began our move to Pleasant Hill. Mother, Phyllis and I made the initial move in 1989. We purchased a 16x80 foot mobile home and moved in onto Pleasant Hill. David had moved to Montgomery to live with Phyllis and me after graduating from high school in Phoenix. He attended Troy State University for a while, then married and moved to Florida for a while before moving near us at Pleasant Hill Farm with his family in 1990.

There were monumental tasks to complete if we were to be successful in reclaiming the old farm. There were fences, barns and workshops to construct and land to be cleared for pastures in addition to the construction of our new home. The task of constructing the home fell on my shoulders. I served as general contractor, a job I had never before attempted, but one I welcomed and enjoyed. We had selected plans for our new home, and we all agreed on the structure. Acquiring subcontractors was most difficult. I interviewed each and selected what I thought was the best of the lot.

Darrell Watson of Tuscaloosa County served as my lead carpenter. He assembled a crew to frame the house and black it in. Major Ernest, a local concrete artisan, did an excellent job in pouring the walls and foundation. The construction project progressed reasonably well, and we moved into the house in 1991, saying goodbye to our mobile home.

I soon discovered that we had just begun work on the farm. It would require literally years to totally reclaim the property. A cousin of mine, S. L. Hall, explained it best. He said that from the day he retired as an over-the-road trucker and returned to his farm, which was just outside the Berry city limits, it took 10 years before he was satisfied with his reclamation project. I believe his time estimate, at least for our farm, was grossly understated. We continue the reclamation of Pleasant Hill Farm to this day. It seems as though there are not enough hours in the day to accomplish all of the work that needs to be done. We are all proud of our efforts, however.

My mother enjoyed several years of being back home in Berry before she passed away suddenly from a stroke at age 87 on September 20, 1997. To say that she is still missed today would truly be an understatement. Phyllis and I miss her each day of our lives. Mother was such a strong influence on my life. I am truly grateful that she was able to enjoy her final years in her beloved home of Berry, and to experience my early years as mayor. Her memory and the impact she had on my life are etched in my heart forever.

Roy and Phyllis Dobbs

The Years Passed Quickly

The years from 1987 to 1992 passed more quickly than I could have ever imagined. I enjoyed only a brief retirement of approximately four years before discovering a second and even most interesting career in local government.

In early 1992, I was approached by several Berry community leaders who asked me to run for mayor of Berry. I was reluctant at first; my political desires were focused more on the state legislature than the town of Berry. At the same time, I realized there were serious problems in Berry, starting with the lack of quality drinking water. That was just one of the local problems and issues that concerned me and drew me into running for the position of mayor.

My dear mother initially pleaded with me not to run. "People will say bad things about you, Son," she argued. I responded, "Mother, we know the truth, and I feel God is directing my efforts; things will be okay." After much prayer, some serious thought, and further discussions with Phyllis and my mother, I proudly accepted the challenge. I soon felt that this was my calling and that I must win if we were to have any hopes of providing the citizens of Berry with any semblance of sound local government. Over the years, God opened doors and made many wonderful things possible for our small town of Berry.

The mayoral campaign of 1992 pitted me against 24-year incumbent Earl Cannon, who had a reputation for somewhat questionable leadership. I was a relative newcomer, having only recently returned to Berry after being away for more than 40 years. Two months before the election, my cardiologist informed me that I had 80 percent blockage in the main artery leading to my heart. His comment was, "Your run for mayor is over. Get something less strenuous to do." I simply responded, "You do your job, and God will make the final decision whether I run for mayor or not."

As I was wheeled toward the operating room, the doctor consoled me with a little encouragement by reminding me that the waiting room was packed with my family and friends, including Mother, Phyllis, our preacher, my son David, and many friends. The doctor moved on to the operating room, leaving me alone on the cold, steel gurney just outside the operating room. I felt somewhat apprehensive to say the least. I was not exactly sure what the outcome was going to be. My doctor had informed me I had a better than 50–50 chance of surviving the operation.

As I lay there totally alone, a warm feeling permeated my body. It seemed as though a glow appeared in that dimly lit room, and I felt the presence of God. These words were given from God: "I am with you, and I will always be with you. You will survive this operation, and you will serve the people. That is My wish, and I will serve with you."

That was not the end of my health problems. Another stumbling block appeared six months down the road after open-heart surgery when I was informed early in my first term that I had prostate cancer and would require a radical operation. Such news could have caused me to just throw in the towel and quit, considering the cancer an omen to not perform my duties as mayor. But to the contrary, I knew that God had a plan for me and as long as I was working His plan everything would work out fine. I am happy to say that both surgeries were successful.

Nine days after my release from intensive care at Druid City Hospital in Tuscaloosa, I was on the campaign trail, going door to door and moving closer to a successful campaign for mayor of Berry.

I won by a wide margin, and installation ceremonies for mayor and five city council members took place on the first Monday evening in October 1992. The swearing in of a new administration ushered in a new era and a new beginning for the town of Berry. Welcomed changes over the next 20 years produced many needed improvements and transformed a once-dying town into a vibrant community again. The people of Berry asked for and supported the many changes and improvements that materialized.

As the new mayor of Berry, I was introduced to a mountain of unforeseen problems. Many of them, including the water situation, required immediate attention, while others demanded financial support that was not available at that time. The challenges were evident; the solutions were not so apparent.

I inquired at the Bank of Berry about the town's financial status, wondering how much money was in the account. I was informed that the town did have a bank account, but only a small amount of money was in the account. Payment was due on a Farmers Home Administration loan that had been acquired to construct the water plant some years before. The amount due for the year was about $45,000. The prior administration had borrowed $45,000 to pay the FHA loan payment for 1991. That sounds like our federal government, borrowing your way out of debt. It doesn't work that way in local government, however.

That was not our only dilemma. There were few records to guide our moving forward, there were mounds of current bills, and the water department was operating at a sizable annual deficit. I could go on, but I believe the circumstances are quite clear. The town of Berry was broke with no visible means of recovery.

How would you like to assume the controls of that runaway train? That's how I felt at the time. Sales tax revenues appeared to be our primary source of revenue, and I felt that the water department should be a positive revenue producer, also.

The Berry Water Department served approximately 800 households, not only in the Berry municipal area but also throughout Fayette County. Though the existing billing structure would not support the debt, much less provide the monthly expenses necessary to maintain the system.

My first few days in office are somewhat difficult to describe since there were so many opportunities and so many problems to face. I knew that the ideal way to solve problems was to prioritize them and solve them one at a time. However, in our case there were so many problems that we had to work on several of them at the same time.

We had dilapidated equipment to maintain our existing crippled water and waste water systems. Our employees were undertrained and grossly underpaid. The employees were without a retirement plan or health insurance coverage. Our maintenance equipment was either worn out or nonexistent, and our streets were in total disrepair. In a nutshell, our little town was dying, and we did not have sufficient revenues to give it the stimulus to survive. I could go on and on and on, but I suspect the aforementioned conditions clearly illustrate our need for change and progress.

Just a few weeks after I assumed the office of mayor, I was asked by Ed Watkins, a reporter for *The Tuscaloosa News*, "Were conditions as bad as you thought, Mayor?" My response to Ed was, "Not at all." He quickly pushed his chair back and said, "I have covered this area for 25 years and you mean things were not bad?" I responded with, "You asked if things were as bad as I had perceived." "That's right," he said. I responded, "Things were much worse than I could have ever imagined. When you are bankrupt and have limited resources, where do you turn?"

Just before being sworn into office, Councilman Jimmy Madison met with Neal Sandlin to try to convince him to return to Berry as our water and street superintendent. Neal had been in Berry for a short time with the prior administration but had become so disappointed with the lack of organization and support that he had resigned.

Jimmy and I made Neal an offer he couldn't refuse. We made him promises, and we never wavered from our commitment to him. Neal made his home in Winfield, and we had such a need for his services that we agreed to allow him to remain in Winfield. The council approved transportation, recognizing that Neal was on call 24 hours a day, seven days a week. Neal never let us down; he proved to be a sound investment and a true asset to Berry.

Council members came and went during the succeeding years, but Jimmy remained in office and was loyal to me and my efforts for my entire 20 years in office. Today Jimmy serves as mayor, having succeeded me upon my retirement.

Much was accomplished during my 20-year tenure as mayor of Berry, but it would be unfair to take all the credit for the many improvements we produced. The advancements were realized through a team approach. Everything was thoroughly discussed with the council, city clerk, water superintendent, chief of police, and our employees. The improvements we made in our town's quality of life will always be near and dear to my heart.

Early in my first term as mayor we hired Marie McClusky, then a recent graduate from the business school at The University of Alabama, to fill the position of city clerk. Marie had been working in a garment factory but wanted to expand her horizons with a more responsible position. She possessed skills in finance and had sound business decision-making abilities, and therefore quickly became a valuable team member.

Our wastewater facility was closely monitored by the Alabama Department of Environmental Management. The system we were using was relatively new, having been installed in 1989, but it was not capable of handling all the extraneous water runoff. We hired what we thought were experts to improve the system, but even after much work the system still did not function effectively. ADEM issued an administrative order that mandated that we, and I as mayor, correct the wastewater problems.

Designing a new system was not difficult, but securing financing for the project was certainly an issue. Thankfully, our congressional representatives in Washington and the Alabama Department of Economic Development assisted us with over $1 million to finance the construction of a new wetlands wastewater facility. The system satisfied ADEM and provided a non-mechanical system that will support Berry for many years.

One large task was behind us, but another one loomed on the horizon. Clean drinking water had for many years been a high priority of mine. Berry was providing water to a large portion of Fayette County, but the water quality was questionable. ADEM was on our case constantly to enhance and clean up our water system. We had the water source, since Berry owned an 80-acre lake known as Bay's Lake.

The town, with financial assistance from the U.S. Department of Housing and Urban Development, had funded the purchase of the lake and also made funds available to replace a faulty dam. Procurement of the lake and the installation of a filter plant in 1976 provided ample drinking water for the area.

The plant had a capacity of 350,000 gallons per day, but it was difficult to manage and operate since it was a total manual operation plant. It was also difficult to maintain, particularly with only one grade-three operator. Correcting this problem required several million dollars. Engineering, acquiring property on which to locate the plant, and construction of a new filtration plant presented a formidable task. They were difficult issues, but not insurmountable. The council and I labored over the problem for many years, but we finally solved the problems and built a new $8 million water plant on a site adjacent to the old water plant after acquiring the necessary land from the Weyerhauser Corporation.

The old water plant was quickly falling behind in water production. In other words, the plant was dying. There was another issue. We had begun to extend drinking water to families throughout the county. There were additional demands not only on the water plant but also on our personnel and equipment. The plant had difficulty providing the necessary volume of water and of the quality needed. It became apparent that a larger, more efficient facility was needed. Hendon engineering in Birmingham, with input from our water superintendent Neal Sandlin, designed a new drinking water facility. The new system was ultimately approved to produce 2 million gallons per day. The new plant was constructed near the old plant on the banks of Bay's lake. The plant with the assistance of four grade-four certified operators produces water for over 1,600 households throughout that county. Total cost of the new plant was $8 million. The financing came from a $5 million loan and a $3 million grant from U.S. Department of Agriculture.

There were other issues as well. During my first administration we dealt with restructuring the water rates. That was essential, and the absence of any records made the task quite difficult. There was the absence of computers to chart and provide viable options. However, if we expected to become financially sound and pay our debt to the FHA then we had to find additional revenues. After we restructured the rates the water department began to support itself.

There were new problems to face every day. We had inherited a rural medical clinic that was without medical service at the time. I asked and received permission from Washington, D.C., to use this building as a City Hall-medical complex. My intent was to move City Hall and maintain half of the building for a future medical clinic. I certainly intended to reopen the medical services as quickly as possible. The need for a medical clinic and a new City Hall was obvious. However, most people felt that the medical clinic would have very little chance to survive because doctors are reluctant to come to small towns.

It took years of work, but we were finally successful in our efforts to reopen the medical clinic in about 2005. Today we have a wonderful nurse practitioner, Dana Norris, who is sponsored by Doctor Gary Fowler of Winfield Alabama. The medical facility is doing well and serving the people of our community as well as the surrounding area.

We also made much-needed improvements, internally and externally, in our city administrative building. We developed and rebuilt the old building, replaced the roof on the City Hall-medical building, and built council chambers. Bill Hammack, a good friend of mine who has since passed on, was instrumental in the design and building of our chambers for the council meetings.

Berry probably has fewer employees than most towns our size, but we have dedicated employees, and we compensate them comparable to other towns or cities larger than ours. We instituted a retirement plan and offered medical insurance (Blue Cross-Blue Shield family plans) for employees. We provided quality training to bring our employees up to speed in all areas as well as the equipment needed to perform work assignments in a safe manner. Also, we constructed a new fire station and purchased a new fire truck.

My most treasured accomplishment was the completion of the Berry Civic Center. In 1999, I was convinced that our small community needed a quality facility that would support our senior citizen program as well as family reunions, weddings, receptions, elementary and high school events, church and civic functions, and almost any other event or function.

I proposed my idea for a community facility. The initial financial support for the Civic Center came from a cousin of mine, S. L. Hall. He, too, perceived this to be an essential addition to our town, and he generously donated $100,000 toward construction of the facility anonymously. Upon his death, he left an additional $400,000 for perpetual care of the center.

Another philanthropist from Fayette, Alabama, Earl McDonald, bequeathed $200,000, which due to delay after his death, resulted in $250,000 for perpetual care of our Civic Center. The contribution from Mr. McDonald came as a result of a dear friend, long-time Fayette Mayor Guthrie Smith, who supported my efforts and served as an important friend and mentor. Mayor Smith had so much faith in our efforts in Berry that he convinced his friend Earl McDonald to leave us at least $200,000. Both gentlemen have passed on, but a great deal of gratitude is due each of them.

The Berry Civic Center was completed and dedicated in 2007. Today, the building is known as the Roy H. Dobbs Building, thanks to action by the Berry City Council in 2012. I deeply appreciate the honor and take a great deal of pride in not only the building but in the town of Berry itself and the progress it has made during the last 20 years.

Opportunity Fulfilled My Destiny

The Birmingham News, *The Tuscaloosa News*, and television station 33/40 in Birmingham produced news articles on my election as mayor with emphasis on my return to Berry. Each questioned my motivation and rationale for even moving to such a small town. Their comments were, "Why would you leave an affluent area of Birmingham to return to Berry?" They felt it couldn't be the money or the prestige. I told them that Berry was my home and that I felt that it was my destiny. I said that I knew God had a plan for my life, and my mission was to help those less fortunate in any way I could.

I never lost sight of that mission during my 20 years as mayor. I knew that with God's direction and the talent with which He had blessed me many wonderful things could and would happen. What did I get out of it? That question has frequently been asked of me. I have simply responded that I was not looking for anything in return. My prior experiences, civic involvements, military affairs, and associations like my years with Governor George Wallace were sufficient to boost my ego for a lifetime.

My reasons for returning to Berry after retirement were somewhat undefined at the outset of the move, but I did feel there was a driving force directing me home. I was unaware of the challenges that lay ahead. I truly did not know what my mission was, but I felt that God did, and He used me and provided the energy and knowledge needed to meet the challenges that our town faced.

In retrospect, the job was a challenge, and at times almost overwhelming, but the results were extremely gratifying. Early on, someone suggested that maybe everyone should have a chance to serve one term as mayor of a small town, and after five terms I can say that 20 years on the job is more than adequate. Maybe term limits would be more desirable, however, it did take the 20 years to solve some of the challenges.

I enjoyed the opportunities I had to serve the people of Berry and help solve the difficult problems that faced us. Developing the personnel and helping them learn more and rise higher was very gratifying. I not only served the people of Berry, but I made many wonderful friends who I will cherish for a lifetime.

When the final chapter is written and my days have long past, I sincerely hope the people of Berry will continue to appreciate the Berry Civic Center, the water treatment plant, the wastewater plant, and the many other lasting things that we developed during my tenure and say that they are happy that God sent Mayor Dobbs back home. I like to think that I fulfilled God's prophecy for me. In Isaiah 6:8, God commanded Isaiah to serve his will. Isaiah responded to God saying "Here I am, Lord, send me," and I believe God gave me the same charge.

I began my 20 years as mayor of Berry on the first Monday evening of October in 1992. It was a milestone in my life, and I discovered the true inner fibers of my soul during my tenure as mayor. Those years are discussed elsewhere in this book.

I am now 81 years old, and I do not know what God will present for the future. But whatever it is, I will be ready and I am confident that God will prepare me for the mission. I hope that when my days are finished on this earth and I approach the gates of heaven God will say, "Welcome, My good and faithful servant. You ran the race. You finished the course. Now here are the treasures I promised you."

My sincere desire is that each person reading this book will do so knowing that we all have a purpose in life. We may not realize exactly what that purpose is, but with God's help, a great deal of perseverance and a tenacious attitude, success can be achieved if one keeps a sharp eye on the goal and never settles for mediocrity.

I don't necessarily believe success is measured in the amount of money that one acquires. I do believe that deep down we all have an innate ability to produce at a higher level than we may initially realize. Possibly some never really understand or visualize just what that level is until later years, some possibly never. I challenge each and every reader not to squander any of the precious time you have because all of our lives are measured in the proverbial hourglass. The sands of time drift away quickly, and we are limited in the amount of time that we have to perform our tasks here on this earth. I hope by sharing my many challenges, accomplishments and failures, I know I have fulfilled my destiny. I have been blessed to know and learn from so many wonderful people in my life.

Motivation to Run for Mayor

I was asked numerous times why in the world I chose to seek the position of mayor in Berry. The answer to that question is still somewhat cloaked in mystery, even to me. I do know that many factors contributed to the decision.

We faced many problems in our return to Pleasant Hill. The first was finding that city water was not available on Pleasant Hill Road. I was informed by neighbors that I would probably need to drill a couple of wells for drinking water. I thought that was ridiculous, since a water main ran along Highway 18 only eight tenths of a mile from our farm. In addition, there were several other homes on Pleasant Hill Road in need of quality drinking water.

I began an almost daily pilgrimage from Birmingham to Berry in the spring of 1988. Since my wife Phyllis was still employed at BellSouth Telephone Company, there was much to be decided and done. I typically arrived in Berry around 7 a.m. and worked all day, making final arrangements for our eventual relocation to Berry.

On one of those many trips to Berry, I sought a meeting with Mayor Cannon regarding the city extending water service to our property on Pleasant Hill. I had made several earlier attempts to meet with the mayor without success and was anxious to resolve my water problem. On this particular morning, I drove into town and parked my 1988 Chevrolet pickup truck in front of City Hall. I was desperate; I did not want to be forced to drill wells on my property for a water supply. I wanted city water.

I had previously agreed to help with the expense of extending the water line from Highway 18 to my property, but the mayor had not received the offer favorably. In fact, he had bluntly informed me that it was not going to happen. In desperation, I decided to locate the mayor and confront him once and for all with my need for city water.

When I entered City Hall, I saw a young lady in the reception area who identified herself as the town clerk. I requested an audience with the mayor. "He is at lunch," she replied. "He is entertaining some important officials from the State of Alabama Military Department." I was positive she could feel the anxiety in my voice as I asked, "Where exactly are they dining?" She gave me directions, and I thanked her and proceeded directly to the restaurant.

I entered the front door of the small restaurant, which had a couple of dining rooms and a semiprivate dining area, where I found the mayor and four military officers in their Army dress green uniforms. When I entered the room I could only see their backs. I approached the mayor and apologized for the interruption, explaining that I had a critical need to discuss with him at a more appropriate time.

"What is it you want?" the mayor asked. Before I could respond, a slightly gray-haired Army colonel named Richard Stone turned and said, "Roy Dobbs, what are you doing in this little town?" I explained that Berry was my home town and that my family and I intended to soon move back to the area. Colonel Stone and I began to discuss our days together with Governor George Wallace in Montgomery when Mayor Cannon interrupted our discussion and asked Colonel Stone, "Do you know this man?" "Certainly," the colonel responded. "Roy Dobbs is a personal friend of Governor Wallace," Colonel Stone said. "As a matter of fact, he is closer to the governor than I am," the colonel added. "He is?" the mayor responded, obviously impressed, and then he asked me again what I wanted to see him about.

"I want city water run to my property on Pleasant Hill; I intend to move my family back here." Mayor Cannon asked when I would need the water, and I told him that we hoped to move in by November. "It [the water] will be there," the mayor quickly responded. Sometimes it is whom you know or simply have someone perceive your importance that really makes all the difference. When we moved to Berry in May 1989 the water was there. We had a two-inch line running from Highway 18 to approximately eight homes on Pleasant Hill Road. The line was not ideal, but it was better than drilling a well.

That wasn't the end of the story. The water provided by the town water system was substandard and often the color and condition of the water was questionable. The water problems we experienced were not ours alone, of course. Approximately 800 households throughout the county were served by the Berry water system, and all were experiencing the same problems. The quality and availability of the water was a mystery. We experienced frequent water outages ranging from a few hours to as much as two weeks.

Three particular influential community leaders encouraged me to enter local politics and thus had a great impact on my life and what became a second career. The process started one afternoon when I received a telephone call from Richard Walker, owner and operator of the Berry Piggly Wiggly food market. Walker said that he, Maurice Manning, principal at Berry Elementary School, and Billy Ray Gurganus, a businessman, would like to meet with me. He said they had a proposal they wanted to discuss with me. I met with them in Walker's office at the Piggly Wiggly, where they each expressed their concerns about the direction of the town and the management style of then-mayor Earl Cannon. Their concern was for the town itself.

They pointed out that the town's water quality was bad at best, the wastewater system was less than desirable, and the police protection was not administered fairly. They wanted me to take those things under consideration and see if there was something I could do to recommend improvements. Those recommendations were nothing short of my seeking the office of mayor. I assured them I would consider all of the things we had discussed and get back with them later. I still had several tasks to complete on my own property.

I met with Sam Henderson, Doug Samford, Owen Sweat, and a few other people about the water system. Sam had a small store and gas station in Roslyn City on Highway 43 north of Berry. They were on the Berry water system, and they also expressed concerns about the water. They agreed that at times the water was unfit for human consumption. We went to Mayor Cannon and asked him to turn the Berry water system over to a qualified water manager, but he refused to do so.

After several other meetings with Mayor Cannon failed to produce any improvements in our water, the committee hired Scott Coogler, an attorney in Tuscaloosa, to help us in the matter. Scott and the committee met with Mayor

Cannon to no avail. The mayor refused to relinquish control of the waterworks, but our efforts did not stop there. We filed legal action in District Court, and Mayor Cannon finally stepped down as water superintendent and sought a qualified replacement.

The mayor hired Neal Sandlin from Winfield to oversee and attempt to correct some of the problems in the water system. Neal was a certified water plant operator with many years of experience. Neal made a concerted effort to correct the problems at the water plant and repair much of the ill-fated distribution lines. The water distribution lines stretched over a large part of Fayette County, going to the Fayette city limits northward and southward to the Tuscaloosa County line.

Sandlin worked virtually alone without additional manpower or the necessary equipment to adequately address many of the problems. Finally, about six months after he was employed by Mayor Cannon, his tenure at Berry came to an abrupt end.

I was present at the September 10, 1990, city council meeting the night that Sandlin resigned. I had been invited to attend the meeting by Don Honeycutt, chairman of the Berry Gas Board, who wanted my support for a proposition that he was going to make regarding the Berry Gas Board. Early that Monday afternoon, I stopped by the City Hall and found

Mayor Cannon standing outside with some other men. I asked the mayor if the regular Monday evening council meeting was still scheduled for 6 p.m. that night. "It is, but why do you want to know?" he asked.

I explained that I was going to attend. "I'm a citizen of Berry, and I felt like I should attend the council meetings," I said, adding that I had been asked by a friend who is on the agenda to be there and support him. "You are not welcome," Mayor Cannon quickly responded. "You are nothing but a troublemaker." "What have I done to you?" I asked him. "The only thing I have been involved in was an attempt along with many others to improve the quality of our drinking water." "You are not welcome and you are not coming," the mayor said emphatically.

Then, more determined than ever to attend the meeting, I said, "Mayor, I am a resident of Berry. You annexed my property into the city limits prior to my returning to Berry, therefore, by law, I can and should be concerned about how my local government is being operated. I will be here unless you change the location without notifying anyone," knowing that such a tactic had been used in the past.

Before 6 p.m. that evening, I entered the small council chambers at the old City Hall. The entire building, which was constructed in 1933 and functioned as City Hall and the city jail with two cells until 1950 was extremely small. One slightly larger room, about 12x20 feet, held a desk and chairs while another smaller room, approximately 9x12 feet, had a desk and a chair that the mayor and clerk shared. The two old jail cells were used to house old records and other materials. The building was totally inadequate to meet the needs of the town.

There was a quorum for the council meeting that evening. Mayor Cannon and council members Wanda Deese, Bobby Pendley, and Calvin Madison were on hand. There were five council members then just as there are today, and three council members and the mayor did constitute a quorum. Two council seats were vacant because two members had resigned.

Others attending the council meeting that particular evening were Neal Sandlin, water manager for Berry; Don Honeycutt, chairman of the Berry Gas Board; Michael James, editor of the Fayette newspaper; and me, of course.

I vividly recall Mayor Cannon seated behind the desk. Councilman Deese was seated in an office chair, while Michael James, Don Honeycutt, and I were seated in metal folding chairs. The other participants were standing or leaning on boxes. Councilman Madison was leaning on an old IBM card sorter. The lighting in the small, crowded room was barely adequate. I had no idea what the evening would be like since it was my initial council meeting, but sparks soon began to fly.

Mayor Cannon began the meeting by telling the council about a letter from the State Mental Health Board asking the council's approval on some matter. It was not clear what the intent of the correspondence was from the mayor's vague interpretation, and the council did not grant its approval. The mayor was visibly upset by the council's refusal to go along with his recommendation and anger spread over his face.

Neal Sandlin was then recognized and given five minutes to address the council. Neal's comments were directed at the mayor. Neal was very upset visibly, and his voice and demeanor revealed his feelings. As he began to speak, his voice quivered and he had a nervous twitch in his speech. He presented several graphic concerns, some of which I recall.

He said he had worked relentlessly day and night, including weekends, in an attempt to solve the many problems he had discovered in the Berry water system. He said he had received little assistance from the mayor, and with the absence of trained employees, most all the work had fallen on his shoulders. The final indictment came when he expressed the lack of concern the mayor had exhibited. He said he had been verbally abused by the mayor and directly accused the mayor of cursing him on several occasions.

"I did not," Mayor Cannon angrily responded, demanding proof. Neal said he could get proof, but it wasn't worth it. Neal felt alone, and without support from the mayor said he could no longer perform his duties. He announced his immediate resignation and stormed out of the meeting visibly disturbed. I did not see Neal Sandlin again until I took office as mayor in 1992.

The council meeting was now in total disarray. Some of us were in shock over Neal's departure. Wanda Deese and Calvin Madison pleaded with Neal to stay. "No way," he responded. Neal was our only hope for resolving the water problems in Berry. I know now that those of us in that room and all who subscribe to water from the Berry system could not have imagined how bad our water situation really was.

I had been sitting on that hard steel chair for quite some time. I leaned over and whispered quietly to Michael James of the Fayette *Times-Record* that my right leg has gone completely numb. Immediately the mayor ceased his dialogue and looked straight at me. "You think this is funny, don't you?" he asked. I responded, "Mayor Cannon, I was not disruptive; I simply shared with Mr. James that my leg had fallen asleep."

"You're nothing but a troublemaker," the mayor quickly responded. "I know what you are doing; you think you're going to run for mayor. I could take the sorriest person in Berry and run against you and beat you." Mayor Cannon went on to call me unappreciative and hypocritical, saying that he had run water to my house and that I had since worked against him. "They ought to throw you out of the church," he added, and these comments are taken directly from the news report of the council meeting as written by Michael James in *The Times-Record*.

The Race for Mayor

The events that took place at that particular council meeting on September 10, 1990, no doubt prompted me to run for the office of mayor. During the next several months I had time to think about it and also canvass the people of Berry to get their feelings. I realized there must be additional problems other than water, although I was confident there were none greater because we all consume water daily and our health depends on good, safe drinking water.

I talked to some of the prominent leaders in our community and with much encouragement from a number of other people in the town, seeking their concerns about our local government. In every case I found their concerns over the drinking water was a paramount issue. Secondly, they wanted to see fair and equitable law enforcement rendered across the board: men, women, boys and girls, with no color barriers. Those are the things I told the people I would address immediately. The time for qualifying for the fall election came in June 1992.

My wife and I talked about it at length, and we also discussed it with my mother. My mother, who had moved back to Berry with us, expressed grave concerns about my running for mayor. "People are going to say bad things about you, Son," she warned. "Mother, you and I know the truth and that's the main thing. People are always going to say some bad things about folks. I really feel like I can serve the people of Berry and that I can make a positive difference in the lives of people in this town." My dear mother said, "You know I'll be praying for you every day that you serve." After the three of us considered all the pros and cons, I decided, with the blessing of my wife and mother, to run for mayor of Berry.

The people of Berry had some genuine concerns. There were many who were reluctant to vote for me for one reason or another. Some told me that Mr. Cannon knew how they voted in past elections and if they voted for me and he were to win that he would know they voted for me and would hold it against them. I assured the people that I would see that we had a voting machine that no one could tamper with and no one could know how they voted. I told the voters that they had the privilege of a secret ballot no matter how they voted. I wanted them to feel good about the election process.

I went before the City Council and asked them to get a voting machine prior to the election to protect the privacy of the votes. The council voted to install the machine and employed poll workers based on their qualifications to work the polls. The pole workers were not my people, and they were not they mayor's people. They were simply concerned citizens who wanted the best for our town, including a fair and honest election.

I visited citizens in their homes and businesses during the campaign. We discussed issues we wanted to improve upon. I constantly asked, "What are your primary concerns for your town?" Without question, the main concern was our drinking water. At the time we were discussing this, I had no earthly idea of the poor financial condition of our town. I told the people that I would do everything in my power to correct the problems in our drinking water production and distribution system. The campaigning began in full force in early June of 1992.

I am not naïve enough to think that the people of Berry loved me that much, but I do believe, and I found out over the next 20 years, that they were desperate for change and that they really understood the need for change. I recall one particular discussion that arose during the campaign. An elderly lady I had known all my life approached me and said, "Roy, you know I can't vote for you and you know why." I told her that I did not know why. "Well," she said, "Earl has always done favors for me and if I vote for you and then he wins, he would cease those special favors for me." I had better judgment than to ask what the special favors were, but I assured this wonderful lady that I intended to win with or without her vote, and that upon my inauguration as mayor of Berry, I would consider her requests along with those of everyone else.

I explained to her that all my actions as mayor would be done legally and ethically and that I would treat everyone fairly, just as I had promised throughout the campaign. I also told her that I would do the very best job I could to make sure that Berry was placed back on the road to prosperity. I'm confident that she didn't vote for me, but as I shared with her, regardless of the way she voted my service was going to be the same for everyone. Several other people made similar comments about Mayor Cannon doing special favors for them during the campaign.

I had my open-heart surgery in June 1992, just before final campaigning for mayor began, and it slowed me down a bit, but not for long. Within nine days after leaving the hospital, I was back on the campaign trail, talking to people and convincing them that we needed change in Berry. The voting took place in August. We had worked hard to register people who were not registered to vote in the town, and we worked hard to get people out to the polls to exercise their right to vote. *The Tuscaloosa News* reported after the fact that the election drew the largest turnout percentage-wise that they had ever witnessed. We had over 690 registered voters in our community and 80 percent of them voted. I received about 78 percent of the vote, winning by a wide margin in defeating the 24-year incumbent mayor.

I feel that Mayor Cannon, who was actually a distant cousin, never recovered from the crushing defeat. He died a short time later. I have sometimes thought that perhaps Mayor Cannon became tired or frustrated in the job after so many years. At the time I was elected, I know for certain that it would have been easy for him to feel overwhelmed by the problems that had accumulated over the years.

I truly believe that my return to Berry was more than a coincidence. I am confident that divine guidance brought me to Berry as someone who could lead the town out of total chaos and financial disaster into prosperity again. And I say that only with the utmost modesty because I know it was more God's doing than my own.

I won the election with an unprecedented voter turnout, and there was an open expression of joy and newfound hope in town as the people realized that we were on the brink of a new horizon. And over the next 20 years, we made great progress with the assistance of many people, including my wife Phyllis, and encouragement from my mother and the guidance of our Lord Jesus Christ. We began a journey with an unknown destination, but the Lord knew and He led the way.

Almost every step of the way was plagued with what might appear to be impossible challenges, but through hard times we never lost sight of what we expected the end result to be. Now at 81 years old, as I look back in retrospect I remember the days that I walked the streets of Berry barefooted with my friends and many of the kids that would come in from the farms on Saturdays. We had some great times in Berry, and I wanted to revive those times and those experiences for the future. I was determined to restore the "good old days" to Berry.

As I have said before, many people asked me why I wanted to become mayor of a town that paid only $100 a month for the job. Honestly, I never really had the desire to run for mayor; my goal was to eventually run for the state legislature. But God had a different plan for my life, and I feel like He fulfilled my life in so many different ways. I am happy to say that I was able to contribute to what Berry is today.

Unexpected Challenges

When I first took office as mayor in October of 1992, it took me day and night, seven days a week, for at least the first year to uncover the vast number of problems, then to develop a plan to address the problems. Most required financial support, which was difficult, to uncover an adequate revenue stream. There was no money in the bank, and the town was $100,000 in debt. Official records were nonexistent. There were few employees, and they lacked the necessary training for their jobs, and certainly I mean no disrespect to them in saying that.

My wife Phyllis along with dear friends and residents of our town Sue Moon and Lavonne Madison, the wife of current mayor Jimmy Madison, worked diligently to locate and sort through the town's outstanding debts, many of which were more than a year delinquent. Obviously, when there is no money in the bank it's difficult to pay the bills. In addition, we had inadequate office space, telephone service, and equipment. Basically, we were starting at square one.

I worked until I was satisfied that I was getting the job done. I didn't count the hours, and I didn't give up. Some people said, "Oh, that can't be done," but my attitude was that it could be done. I saw opportunities for improvement and worked toward our goals. I know I was never afraid of failure. I had learned through the years that failure wasn't fatal, that it was just a point at which to start again.

I'm not the smartest man in the world; I'm just who I am, but I'm not reluctant to try something, to step out and step up to a challenge. If I see a need, I try to find a way to meet that need. Some people lack vision; they can't see beyond the task to the possibilities and results that lie ahead. But I believe that anyone can step out of his or her normal personality, modify his or her behavior, and accomplish great things. You must put on your work boots, step forward, and address the problem head on.

There is one story related to this that my wife enjoys telling. Shortly after I took office as mayor, the water plant called and said they needed some chemicals. I asked where we got the chemicals and was referred to Sipsey Supply, a building and farm supply store in Fayette that could provide the needed chemicals.

Phyllis and I got into our personal 1988 Chevrolet pickup truck and proceeded directly to Fayette. We loaded up several pounds of the chemicals and instructed the company to bill the Town of Berry Water Department. I'll never forget the response of the individual at Sipsey Supply. "Sir, I don't know who you are, the mayor or whomever, but Berry doesn't pay their bills, so we will not send the bill to Berry."

Fortunately I had my personal checkbook on me and wrote a check out for $180 to the Sipsey Supply for the chemicals. That was only the beginning of the story. We had no office furniture. To declare that the old City Hall was small would be an understatement. The main room was 12x20 feet and included the mayor's office and the meeting room for council meetings. The clerk had a small 9x12 office equipped with a single-line black telephone. There were two jail cells that were no longer used to house inmates. Thus, City Hall was totally inadequate to meet the needs of the town.

Shortly after my election, I sought a new location for City Hall. The Berry Gas Board was housed in a building more suitable and had some space to spare. I requested and received permission from the board chairman to move into the gas board building. Later the City Hall was moved to a much larger location, and the new City Hall is close to the Civic Center.

We had received word that the Northport Chamber of Commerce was merging with the West Alabama Chamber serving both Tuscaloosa and Northport and had office furniture for sale. Phyllis and I went down and looked it over. There were desks, chairs, a conference table, and many other items. We purchased $350 worth of furniture, and you can guess where the payment came from. You got it, out of our personal checkbook. We paid for the furniture, loaded it on our truck, and headed back to Berry. We also went to the state government surplus equipment in Montgomery later and purchased desks and chairs to fill our needs at City Hall. Later, when the town was able, we were reimbursed for the furniture. I'm not sure if we were ever paid for the water plant chemicals, but the story is worth the investment.

It would be somewhat difficult for anyone to comprehend just how bad the conditions were in Berry when we took over as mayor. When I say "we" took over as mayor, I am speaking of myself, my wife, the council and employees, because "we" are what it's all about. The mayor would be ineffective alone. A team approach is essential in any organization. When you surround yourself with competent, dedicated associates, the results are usually magnified.

The early years were riddled with strife and struggle. We were sharing office space in an old doublewide trailer owned by the Berry Gas Board. On one occasion, I had a visit from a nurse who had been assigned to our medical center in Berry. The facility had closed prior to her visit. Her comment was, "Mayor, you need to go up to the rural medical building and check on the conditions; they are deplorable. The ceilings are falling in; there are leaks in the roof and it needs repair."

I told her that the building did not belong to the town of Berry. It was a rural medical clinic established by the federal government, and I told her that I would have to call Washington, D. C., to see what I could do about the situation. I called Dr. King in with the Appalachia Region Commission in Washington and asked if Berry's city government could share the building. I provided him a quick rundown on the condition of the building and pledged to work relentlessly to attract medical assistance for our town. He quickly gave us permission to move forward with the move into the medical center, which offered a newer, much larger space that would give us the ability to function better. I kept my commitment to Dr. King, of course.

We had a newer City Hall, but we were still digging our way out of the financial problems that we faced. After Phyllis, Sue and Lavonne discovered just how much money we owed and to whom we owed it, I composed a letter informing our creditors that we would pay all we owed, and we did. Our best estimate was that the town owed just over $100,000, which was a large amount. The obvious question is how we managed to pay off that enormous debt. We restructured our water system billing, analyzed our sales taxes, and reviewed business licenses. The result was a tremendous increase in taxes and a new revenue stream.

The next major challenge came after we had completely analyzed our problems at the water plant and in the water distribution. We then had to decide what we were going to do. We had gotten Neal Sandlin back in Berry, although it was not easy. But we made a commitment to him and he made a commitment to us, and over the 20 years we both honored our commitments. We were able to acquire some much-needed grants from the Alabama Department of Economic Development and from our state senator, Roger Bedford.

A short time before taking office as mayor, Phyllis and I drove to Montgomery and requested that the state perform an audit on the finances of the town of Berry. I told them I had concerns regarding possible misappropriation of money during the prior administration and that I certainly wanted a clean slate on which to begin my term as mayor. I was quickly told that the state auditor's office had much bigger fish to fry than those found in Berry and that I should not expect an audit. That news was both surprising and discouraging, and it left me with the realization that we simply had to pull ourselves out of our financial quagmire on our own.

Our next stop in Montgomery was the Farmers Home Administration, where we met with Bill Summerall, the FHA director for Alabama at the time. I informed Mr. Summerall about our crippled water system in Berry, mentioning the failing raw water pumps and the general dilapidated conditions of our filter plant. I pleaded for some assistance from FHA to help solve the problems. Mr. Summerall was sympathetic, but said there was no grant money available at the time. I made a last-ditch plea for him to please check, telling him I was confident that he could find some money somewhere to help us out of our difficult situation.

A few days later, Mr. Summerall called me with some surprisingly great news. He said, "Would $50,000 help you?" I thanked him profusely and with that $50,000 we made some badly needed repairs to our drinking water plant that helped us avoid a possible shutdown. During the same telephone call, Mr. Summerall asked, "Mayor, what is the status of the water project pending for County Road 26?" He said that project had been on hold for several years and he would like to get it off his books.

He asked me to look at the pending project, which we did, and found that $350,000 had been appropriated for the project. We also determined that to complete the project we would need an additional $300,000, since several years had passed, and I reported our findings to Mr. Summerall. I also told him that we wanted to complete the project because there were about 50 households along the route that had been promised water years ago. Somehow, Mr. Summerall and his staff came through with the additional $300,000 in FHA funds and we were able to begin the final stages of engineering on the project.

As I was canvassing potential customers along County Road 26, seeking their signatures and final agreement to hook onto the new water line, I knocked on a door and a lady answered. I introduced myself, explained that I was the mayor of Berry and that we were getting ready to extend drinking water to the area. "Are you interested?" I asked.

She looked me straight in the eye and said, "Mayor Dobbs, do you know how many times we have been promised water and paid deposits and nothing has happened? Do you really think we will get water in my lifetime?" I said, "Ma'am, I can't promise that you or even I will live until tomorrow, but I promise you that by the end of this year you will have water," and that promise was kept. The completion of the County Road 26 project made the FHA and all the new water customers happy, thanks to Bill Summerall's outstanding assistance. Mr. Summerall retired not too long afterward, but I will always be grateful to him for his genuine willingness to help our area in a time of dire need. The project showed what can be done when people work together, and I emphasize the word work, with an attitude of helping others.

I think that project helped me realize fully the importance of the job I had to do as mayor.

It helped me realize that we were not just dealing with projects and money; we were serving the needs of the people. I never took my job for granted for a single minute after that.

The County Road 26 water project was one of many we completed over my 20 years in office, but it is one that I remember quite well because I had the opportunity to work closely with the people in our area and the people in Montgomery. By working together, we made a difference in the lives of many people. I grew from the experience because it gave me a sense of pride and elevated my confidence as I faced many other problems ahead of us in Berry.

The road to total recovery was a bumpy one, a tough one, and at times it seemed almost insurmountable. But we never gave up and we never lost sight of our objectives. We were able to employ an outstanding administrative grant writer from Huntsville, Terry Acuff, of Community Consultants Incorporated. Terry is an outstanding grant writer and project administrator, and he became a real friend and business partner. When we identified a problem, Terry was there on the spot to help us determine how funds could be secured to address that problem, and God knows there were many needs and problems to be resolved.

There were water projects, sewer projects, street projects, and building a new storm shelter, a walking trail, and a new Civic Center. Terry was an integral part of all of those projects, and I would be remiss if I didn't mention an $8 million water plant and a $2 million waste water facility. Terry provided guidance and support on many of those projects. He was instrumental in putting the ideas on paper and assisting us in seeking finance support for the projects.

We made what I consider outstanding progress during my first four-year term as mayor. We restructured our water billing system, paid off the $100,000 debt, established a larger City Hall in the trailer with the gas board, rehired Neal Sandlin, bought a new backhoe, and accomplished a few more things. I was feeling pretty good about things and probably was a little prideful as I campaigned for re-election for a second term. One of our citizens brought me down to earth one afternoon when I approached him working in his garden and asked for his vote.

"I'll sho' vote for you," he said. "That fella in there now ain't doin' nothin'." That encounter was a lesson in humility. It showed me that at least some of our citizens weren't really aware of the problems we faced or what we had accomplished. I knew then that my work was far from finished, and that I had to work harder to inform and involve as many of our citizens in the process as possible.

Berry Gas Board Changes

The Berry Gas Board, a municipal corporation, was established to provide natural gas to homes and businesses in the area. The gas board served approximately 400 customers at its peak, but gas prices increased over the years, causing the customer base to decline by nearly 50 percent and making the corporation a liability rather than an asset.

During my time as mayor, I became a member of the gas board's board of directors with chairman Billy Ray Gurganus and fellow member Larry Moore. Billy Ray had been a member of the board when the corporation was originally created. I later became chairman of the board while serving with Vice Chairman Calvin Madison and fellow board member Tom Ellard. We carefully reviewed gas service operation and viability and decided that we either had to expand the customer base in order to become profitable or look at other alternatives.

One option was to sell the Berry gas company. We solicited several companies, including Alabama Gas Corporation, who had previously expressed an interest, but they failed to respond. I made a proposal to the Fayette Gas Board, which had recently extended its service from Fayette to near where our existing system ended, making a possible interconnection easily feasible. Merrill Nolen of the Fayette Gas Board expressed interest in the idea, and I consulted with Calvin and Tom, and we made a proposal for Fayette to consolidate the Berry gas system into the Fayette system.

Such as association with the Fayette system would maintain gas service in the Berry area and relieve the Berry Gas Board of the responsibility to maintain the lines and service at a net loss to the city. The plan assured Berry's customers of uninterrupted service and also allowed the town of Berry to receive a franchise fee after a reasonable time. It was truly a win-win situation for all parties concerned. Fayette accepted the offer, and the Fayette Gas Board now serves the Berry area. We have a wonderful working relationship and there is a mutual benefit for both the Fayette and Berry gas customers.

The lesson here is that one should continually evaluate the conditions of an existing company or organization to clearly understand the existing financial and employee circumstances. One can then determine what is best for all concerned. In our case, it included the company (Berry Gas Board), the customers, and the proposed buyer. We all did just that and all parties were satisfied in the end. Not all situations can be improved upon, but it never hurts to review and evaluate policies and procedures in business and government because economic conditions are always changing, and I felt like I was obligated to give my employees and citizens the best possible return on their money and efforts.

Civic Center
Fulfilled a Dream

I had shared my dreams of a Civic Center for our small town with a lot of people, but the very first to share and truly believe in my dream was a cousin, S. L. Hall. S. L. lived just outside of Berry but always considered Berry his home. He and my mother were first cousins.

S. L. summoned me to his house one morning in the fall of 1999 with a proposition. He told me that he knew I was honest and had a good heart and that he, too, wanted the people of Berry and the surrounding area to have a community center. "I know you will do what you say and protect the investment," he added, although at the moment he said that I had no investment to protect.

Then S. L. said, "I want to make the first contribution to your civic center, but I don't want anyone to know who made the contribution until after my death." He then offered the astounding donation of $100,000 toward the building of the Civic Center. He did even more by bequeathing approximately $400,000 at the time of his death, making his total contribution $500,000. The main auditorium in the Civic Center is named the S. L. Hall Auditorium in his honor.

Thanks to S. L. Hall's initial $100,000, $250,000 from Earl McDonald of Fayette, $200,000 from Senator Roger Bedford, $250,000 from Governor Bob Riley, $50,000 from the State Department of Tourism and others, we found the funds to build the Berry Civic Center. The building opened in 2007 and was named the Roy H. Dobbs Building by the Town Council in 2012, giving me a great sense of pride in what I consider a major contribution to our town.

Special Honors

I was quite surprised, humbled and honored to receive the West Alabama Regional Council's David M. Cochrane Award on December 29, 1995, even before I had completed my first term as mayor. This award recognizes a public official each year from our seven-county district who best symbolizes outstanding service and leadership.

The late Guthrie Smith, who served as mayor of Fayette 1955–1992 and who as a true friend and mentor assisted and supported me in every way possible, nominated me for the award and spoke highly of me and the progress we had made in Berry.

"In all my 44 years of municipal government, I have never witnessed a three-year record like that of Mayor Dobbs," Mayor Smith said. "When he took over as mayor in 1992 there was utter chaos at City Hall. He found the city $100,000 in debt; the water department was losing money; the National Guard was hauling water to keep schools and industry operating; there was inadequate sewage disposal; past financial records were non-existent; there was no budget and no records with which to prepare a budget," he added.

"Within three years after Mayor Dobbs took office, the town of Berry was able to pay all its bills on time, budget controls were in effect, and the town government had been placed on a sound financial basis," Mayor Smith added in securing the Cochrane Award for me. Needless to say, I was both proud and flattered by his comments.

Mayor Smith was complimentary of my work in Berry on other occasions as well, including comments made in a letter to the editor of the Fayette *Times-Record* in September 2006. "Mayor Roy Dobbs is a living example of the axiom, 'The purpose in life is to make a difference'," Mayor Smith wrote in the letter. "It is remarkable that instead of retiring from a successful business life, Mayor Dobbs chose to step forward and lead his home town out of utter chaos. I commend him for his superb leadership and all Berry citizens for their continued loyal support. He has indeed made a difference in the lives of all his fellow citizens," he added.

In commenting on the completion of the Berry Civic Center, Mayor Smith said the facility "was the culmination of a long-time dream of Mayor Roy Dobbs. He did not just dream. He worked long and hard to convert that dream into reality. The key to Berry's success story is great leadership, hard work and dedication, which builds confidence in those who can help reach goals," Mayor Smith proclaimed in praising the progress that had been accomplished in Berry made during my first 14 years in office.

Mayor Smith was an inspiration to all who knew him, and he further inspired me by giving me a copy of an anonymous poem entitled "The Beatitudes of a Leader." That essay is worth repeating, and should inspire others as it has me.

"Blessed is the leader who has not sought the high places but who has been drafted into service because of his ability and willingness to serve.

"Blessed is the leader who knows where he is going and how to get there.

"Blessed is the leader who knows no discouragement and who presents no alibies.

"Blessed is the leader who knows how to lead without being dictatorial; true leaders are humble.

"Blessed is the leader who seeks the best for those he serves.

"Blessed is the leader who leads for the good of the most concerned and not for the personal gratification of his own ideas.

"Blessed is the leader who develops while leading.

"Blessed is the leader who marches with the group and interprets correctly the signs on the pathway that leads to success.

"Blessed is the leader who has his head in the clouds but his feet on the ground.

"Blessed is the leader who considers leadership for service."

Mayor Smith began his governmental service as a city councilman in Fayette in 1948 and became mayor in 1955. He retired in 1992 after 44 years of civic service to his community and died in May 2010 at age 97.

I received perhaps my highest honor on June 27, 2013, when the West Alabama Mayors Association established the Roy Dobbs Lifetime Achievement Award in my honor and presented me with the first award at a special meeting. The award is to be given to deserving past and active mayors who have contributed significantly to their city or town through outstanding leadership. I am grateful and truly humbled to have been so honored by my fellow mayors and my sincere hope is that the award will serve as an incentive to others.

Help Came from Many Sources

There were other individuals and political entities that provided financial assistance to Berry in many areas, and another individual was Richard Shelby, the U.S. Senator representing our district in Washington. I met with Senator Shelby and explained to him the problems we were having with our waste water facility and the conditions that existed between Berry, Lake Tuscaloosa, and the city of Tuscaloosa, which is his home. He was extremely interested in our problems and in my proposal for solving the problems.

I explained to Senator Shelby that it was going to take at least $1.5 million to purchase the land and construct a new waste water facility. His commitment was $1 million of that, and he said that he would personally move the request through Congress. The Republican Congress was in control and he chaired the Finance and Appropriations Committee, so I had no doubt that I would get the money. But my luck did not hold out completely. At about the same time we were to receive the $1 million the Iraq war broke out and President Bush cut appropriations by 10 percent. That meant we would get only 90 percent of the million dollars, or $900,000.

Before we could get the money from the Environmental Protection Agency, which was channeling the money to us, another catastrophe came along and the amount was cut again. Ultimately, we got $750,000 of our million dollars, which was still a big help, and I do appreciate Senator Shelby's efforts in helping us with the funding.

We were short a few hundred thousand dollars, so we called on Terry Acuff of Community Consultants to ask if he had any ideas on how we could augment the $750,000. Terry suggested that we apply through the State of Alabama for federal funds and we did so with success. We received a half million dollars, pushing our total to $1,250,000.

The waste water treatment project took several years in designing, pulling all the money together, getting it ready for bids, etc. Then, like everything else at that time, we were at the highest time for fuel prices and the costs continued to rise while our money remained constant. We finally got the system designed, bid and installed, and a lot of credit goes to Senator Shelby, U.S. Representative Robert Aderholt, and the Alabama Department of Economic Development.

One might say that's enough problems for anyone, but that was not the last problem we faced. We had solved the waste water problem and had satisfied to some degree Tuscaloosa mayor Al DuPont, who had been convinced that Berry was polluting Lake Tuscaloosa with its small waste discharge several miles upstream from Lake Tuscaloosa.

I have an odd, somewhat funny story involving Mayor Al DuPont and myself. We are very good friends, and I think the world of him. I once said to him, "Mayor, you need to check those big, expensive homes built on those hills all around Lake Tuscaloosa. They have septic tanks, not city sewer, and their waste water is most likely going directly into Lake Tuscaloosa." I added that there were also many farm animals, chicken houses, and the like in the area that added to the pollution of the lake, which provides drinking water for the city of Tuscaloosa.

My argument fell on deaf ears because I think Tuscaloosa wanted to try to avoid the local issues and blame the problem on the town of Berry, which in the end wasn't the case. But we did solve our problems with waste water. I suggested to Mayor DuPont once that he could help solve the problem that day by giving Berry about $2 million. "I can't give you $2 million," he stuttered. "And I can't solve the problem today either." But we did solve the problem. It just took a little time and a lot of determination and assistance.

The next major undertaking was the drinking water facility. The existing plant had been installed in the 1970s, and Berry had outgrown its capacity. Maximum production was 350,000 gallons a day, and we were at that capacity. The City Council was faced with a real dilemma about what to do. We could not expand the old plant. It was built in such a way that it could not be added onto or improved upon. There were many features of the dilapidated plant that were totally decayed, creating a difficult situation for our water production.

We talked to a number of water systems, including Birmingham, about providing water for Berry. All of them supported our building a new plant. They said that we should, if possible, provide our own water and not depend on someone else. I checked with Fayette about running water from their system over to Berry, but that presented a number of not insurmountable but still difficult problems. One of the problems was that Fayette is lower than Berry, and the water would have to be pumped 24 hours a day, seven days a week, 365 days a year. There would also have been a change in the direction of our water flow, which would have created a problem for descaling the insides of the pipe.

Purchasing water from another city would also take the control of our system away from us and make us totally dependent on another provider. We would be at the mercy of another water system, and if that city found itself short of water due to a drought or other unforeseen problem we could be cut off. I had grave concerns that Berry would not always have the water it needed.

After considering the options, the town council voted to construct a new water plant. We already owned an 80-acre lake, so we had the water. A new water plant was all we needed. The plant was designed to cost $4 million. We petitioned to the U.S. Department of Agriculture's Rural Development Agency for funds, with the majority of it being grant money in combination with a small loan. The struggle to construct the water plant went on and on and on for years. We finally were able to get all the plans together and acquired the financing, or at least we thought we had. The cost of construction had gone up exponentially. When we had the pre-construction bidding for the plant, 10 companies expressed interest in bidding. But in the end, only one company out of Atlanta made a bid, and that bid was almost double what our engineer expected.

Four years earlier, the USDA had asked us to reconsider the plans and cut out areas that we could in an effort to reduce construction costs. We did just that. Though we felt like we were really jeopardizing a lot of the needed features, we reduced our plans, trimming the cost by almost $1 million. We were instructed to re-bid, which we did. Again, only one company came back with a bid and that was the company from Atlanta. This time not only had we lost a great deal of our new plant, but we had compromised more than dollars. Because of rising costs, we were right back at the $8 million figure.

The state director for the USDA personally gave me permission to go ahead and accept the new bid, saying that he would get additional grant money from the Secretary of Agriculture and some more loan money to match. I had performed a special study on our service area, and it again indicated that our water customers were of low to moderate income based on the 2000 census. That meant we qualified for a 75 percent grant and a 25 percent loan.

The USDA came back and said that it could not provide additional grant money but could lend us $5 million. The $3 million grant and $5 million loan was totally reversed. It should have been at least a $5 million grant with a $2 million or $3 million loan, and we had already accepted the contract. We were forced to restructure our water rates to reflect the unexpected additional USDA loan. We had already proven that we were in a low-to-moderate-income area, so we knew that the necessary water rate increase was going to place a financial hardship on many of the families in our area. It was going to be difficult, but living without water was certainly more difficult.

We installed the system, and the year before I left office for the first time ever we had gotten out of the doghouse with the Alabama Department of Environmental Management. We were now recognized as the outstanding plant for 5 million gallons a day and under in the state of Alabama. That is something of which I am truly proud. Our hard working associates at the plant and our maintenance people earned and deserved that award, when just a short few years ago we had received only condemnation. All these things go back to square one when the people of Berry asked me to step up to the plate, be their mayor, and help them out of the numerous bad situations we were in.

Did I know how bad it was when I took it over? No. Did I shy away from the responsibilities? No. Did I ever have any doubts that I had done the wrong thing by seeking the job? Yes, but that did not deter my efforts from fulfilling what I felt like was my destiny to perform the job at the very highest level.

God had blessed me with the necessary training, knowledge, connections and support to get the job done and placed me in that position. I also had the support of my wife Phyllis and the City Council throughout my 20 years in office, and I am thankful for that. I am also thankful for the opportunity that I had to serve the people Berry. Many people asked me just before and after I departed the office of mayor if I thought I would miss it. I said, "Yes, I'll miss some aspects of the job."

Will I miss those calls late at night complaining about potholes in the street or dogs running in the street? Yes, because that's part of the job. I asked for the job of mayor and was elected. I asked for the support of the people, and I received it throughout my tenure. In turn, I did my best and I am proud of what I accomplished in 20 years. I feel that I can look back with pride and say that I rose above mediocrity. I performed at my very highest level. I am proud of my performance. I am pleased and satisfied with the results of our efforts.

I greatly appreciate the support and assistance from all the people who worked with me over the 20 years I served as mayor of Berry to make it a better town and a more viable community. I know I could not have accomplished anything at all without them and the citizens of Berry. We need industry to come into our area to help support our community and to provide jobs for our citizens, and we must never lose sight of the fact that we must continue to work toward that goal. Had we given up in 1992 and said there is no hope, simply let the little town die, that would have been an indictment against our city council, my convictions, and myself. Come visit us in Berry today and see the difference 20 years of work can make.

The mayor of the small Walker County town of Parrish visited me just before I left office and asked me if I would share with him my success story. His comment was, "I have visited Berry over the past 20 years and Berry looked 20 years ago much like my town looks today. If you would, just share with me all the things you did and how you did them so I might be able to do the same things in Parrish."

I did that with the sincere hope that it will encourage him and enlighten him to affect some of the same changes in his community that we did in Berry. There are a lot more adventures in the book, and I am excited to share all of them with the readers. This was just one of the days in the life of a small-town mayor.

Senator Bedford Answered our Call

Roger Bedford, our area state senator from Russellville, deserves special recognition for his assistance to me and to the town of Berry during my tenure as mayor. It mattered not whether our problem was the extension of a water line to a few households down a little, dusty county road or a large network of subscribers on the water system Roger was always there to help. There are many examples of his assistance that I could mention, but I will only share a few.

Some years ago when Berry constructed a new high school gymnasium, Bedford was running for re-election and attended a political rally at the new school gym on a hot, steamy evening. My duties had taken me out of town, and I was unable to attend that particular rally. Upon my return, Nancy Shepherd a member of the Fayette County Board of Education, informed me of a promise that Senator Bedford had made at the Berry rally. She told me that Roger had said, "If the good people of Berry help me get re-elected to the state senate, I assure you that I will get this gym air conditioned."

Roger was re-elected with ease, and holding true to form, Mrs. Shepherd called Senator Bedford's hand, asking him to live up to his promise and provide funding for air conditioning the Berry High School gymnasium. Roger tried to wiggle out of the promise by telling Nancy that she, being in politics, should certainly understand that one cannot always come through on every promise made in the heat of an election campaign. Nancy called me and pleaded with me to use my influence with Senator Bedford to secure the $36,000 needed for the air conditioners. I asked Nancy what exactly Senator Bedford promised. She said, "Senator Bedford said that if the people of Berry would help re-elect him he would assure us that that gymnasium would be air-conditioned and we wouldn't have to sit here in sweat like we are tonight."

I immediately called Senator Bedford and said, "You made a promise and you must keep it." Roger began with, "Roy, you know you can't keep every political promise you make." I countered, "I know, Roger, but this one you must keep. Come up with the money and do this for Berry High School." He did it; he came up with the $36,000, and it made a lot of difference in our small town. A promise is a promise as far as I am concerned, and it's only good if it's kept.

I must share another story pertaining to Roger. Fayette County had 13 volunteer fire departments in the county, and when they held their district meetings Roger would always attend. One of the fire chiefs once complained to Senator Bedford, "Roger, we don't understand why Mayor Dobbs always gets the money he wants and we don't get any." "How many times have you called me or written me a letter?" Senator Bedford responded. The fire chief said, "Well, we just assumed that you wouldn't help us or you couldn't." Roger said, "Mayor Dobbs never quits calling. He never quits writing. He never gives up. He stays on me all the time and that's the kind of prodding it takes. You have to let us know what specific help you need." I supported Roger Bedford during my 20 years in office and Senator Bedford supported me, and I'm proud to call Roger and his family my friends.

Senator Bedford always kept his promises as far as I was concerned. I don't know of a single time that I asked for his help that he did not go all out to help me. Roger and I had an understanding. I believed in him, and he believed in me. More than that, we both believed in helping the people in the Berry area, the county, and throughout his senatorial district. I could share with you many times that Roger assisted us. He helped find funding to build new ball fields and extend water lines and with financing several other projects during my 20 years as mayor. But my most memorable event for both Roger and me came during the planning and construction of the Berry Civic Center.

I had made unsuccessful attempts for several years to construct a Berry community center, or civic center. I had applied for state government grants to whomever I could get to listen to me and to the federal government as well. We had raised a considerable amount of money, and I had asked the governor for consideration in approving a grant that I had pending with the Alabama Department of Economic Development.

"I'm not asking you to do anything illegal, just sign the piece of paper," I told the governor. "The State Department of Economic Development has already told me that our application is most deserving of any in the state of Alabama," I added. But my pleading again fell on deaf ears, and I came away empty handed. I contacted Roger about the problem, and he said, "You are not going to go down in defeat if I can help it." A short time later I received a check in the mail from the Department of Economic Development in the amount of $200,000 to go toward the construction of the Berry Civic Center.

Senator Bedford's comment was, "I was never going to let you down. This project was not going to fail." A new administration and a new governor of Alabama signed the $250,000 grant application, pushing us over the top. We had reached the magic amount of $1.5 million. What had seemed to some as only a pipe dream six years before finally became a reality, and Roger Bedford was instrumental in helping make my dream for the Civic Center a reality.

If I were starting my tenure as mayor again today, I would hope that I had a friend in high places like Roger Bedford. I am grateful to have had the opportunity to work with him; he came through for us many times in difficult situations.

Other Agencies Helped

Early in my first year as mayor I realized I must seek outside assistance to help dig me out of the sinking sand I had stepped into.

I was not familiar with the various agencies and just what assistance, particularly financial assistance, that might be available to small towns like Berry when I took office in 1992. However, I quickly discovered the West Alabama Regional Council in Northport and the Alabama League of Municipalities. Both of these agencies possessed a storehouse of knowledge and expressed willingness to assist my town and me as we sought their assistance.

These two agencies were established to assist municipal governments. The West Alabama Regional Council serves seven counties in West Alabama, with Fayette County being one of those seven counties. Berry had apparently been a member of these organizations at one time but was not a member at the time I assumed the office of mayor.

I discovered that the advice and services provided by these agencies could be critical to Berry and would be well worth the small amount of annual dues Berry would have to pay. We re-established our membership, and over the next 20 years the West Alabama Regional

Commission and League of Municipalities played important roles in the progress of our small town.

I served on the Board of Directors of the West Alabama Regional Council and was elected chairman of the board twice. I participated in many worthwhile programs sponsored by the council. I had an opportunity to develop relationships with state and federal government agencies that proved beneficial for generating much-needed financial support for our small town.

I also served on the Community Services Programs of West Alabama Board of Directors for several years. My association with the other board members and especially the executive director, Cynthia Burton, was educational and enjoyable. The organization filled so many needs of the low-income families of our area. Cynthia and the CSP Board deserve a special word of thanks for their continued outstanding service to West Alabama.

Robert (Bob) Lake was selected executive director of the West Alabama Regional Council on the retirement of Lewis McCray. Bob had been mayor of Moundville for a number of years and came to his position with a great deal of experience and knowledge about local government. Bob and I, along with his wife Linda and my wife Phyllis, worked hand-in-hand for many of those 20 years in a concerted effort to improve services to local governments and the citizens of West Alabama.

Another vital member of the team was the Alabama League of Municipalities, located near the state capitol, in Montgomery. As mentioned before, Berry was not a member of the league when I took office. I feel that my predecessor could have benefited from the advice and assistance of both these organizations had he so chosen.

My initial exposure to the League of Municipalities came early on in my administration. I called Perry Roquemore, executive director of the league, seeking his professional advice. I was confident that Perry had the answers. Not only was he the executive director of the league, he was also an outstanding attorney in the area of municipal law. Over the years, my association with the Alabama League of Municipalities proved to be quite beneficial to me and therefore to Berry. I enjoyed working with Perry and his wife, Suzanne.

I served as a member of the league's executive committee for many years, moderating sessions at the league's annual convention. I was elected vice president of the league for 2008 and 2009, then elevated to president of the league for 2009 and 2010. The many programs and training opportunities offered by the League of Municipalities were very helpful and provided a vast amount of information and solutions for any sized government entity.

During my last term as mayor, Perry Roquemore retired and deputy director Ken Smith was elevated to the position of executive director. Ken, like Perry, was a highly competent attorney and possessed a vast knowledge on municipal government policies and procedures. I enjoyed working with Ken and his wife, Brenda.

These two organizations were created primarily to provide assistance to all municipal governments in Alabama. I feel they both more than fulfilled their charters during my tenure as mayor and contributed greatly to my success.

It was evident early on that I could not be a successful mayor without the help of others. I received assistance from a large number of people, including the Berry City Council; city clerk Marie McCluskey; water superintendent Neal Sandlin; my wife, Phyllis; the citizens of Berry; our Congressional delegation in Washington; our state government representatives; multiple governors of Alabama; state government agencies; the League of Municipalities; and the West Alabama Regional Council.

When I took office as mayor of Berry, I knew from past experience that without teamwork success would be difficult to achieve.

I also knew that any team must be well informed and well trained with clearly defined goals. I knew there had to be a committed leader to provide momentum to successfully attain the desired results. I knew we needed a sound plan and the commitment to complete the plan successfully. I believe we initiated and sustained that required level of teamwork in Berry throughout my tenure as mayor.

It would be difficult for me to offer a definition for success for everyone. I do believe that my success as mayor of Berry was preordained. As I have said before, I really had no idea why I was returning to Berry. I certainly did not intend to run for the position of mayor. But when I was given the opportunity I had a powerful feeling that this was my destiny. I had a deep feeling in my heart that I had an opportunity to do something for someone else.

Our little community was not blessed with a great deal of financial strength. We have many people in Berry surviving on very low to moderate incomes. I realized that God had given me the opportunity and equipped me with the ability, the experience, and the formal education required to handle the job.

I accepted the challenge with the desire to do just that. I found many opportunities to improve the quality of life in our community. Those challenges did not come without a great deal of work and sacrifice, not only for me but for my wife and my family. We gave whatever we had to give, and we walked the path that we had to walk. Remembering a lesson my mother taught me as a youngster to not look backward: Yesterday's opportunities are gone forever. We only looked forward to where we were going.

If one looks back to where he or she has been, most likely he or she will find him or herself stumbling and falling over obstacles that are placed strategically in one's pathway. I found myself removing those obstacles while addressing the needs of the day and persevering toward the goals of the final destination. It would have been very easy just to say, "This is too difficult" or "This is not my fight." I could have acquiesced and just let someone else solve the problems, saying that I did not create them. I recognized, however, that we walk into situations sometimes where we didn't create the problem but are given the opportunity to solve the problem for the benefit of others, and that is how I viewed the opportunity to serve as mayor of Berry.

I genuinely hope that those who read this book will realize that it is easy to quit, blame someone else, or simply say, "I didn't create the problems, so I'm not going to worry about them." But if you do that you really miss the satisfaction of accomplishing a job that perhaps no one else wanted to do or could have done.

I look back now on the 20 years and reflect on all the problems we initially had and remember all the time acquired to address and solve those problems. I have also had an opportunity to talk with people who came up to me after my tenure and said, "Mayor, thank you. Thank you for providing us with good drinking water." Others have said, "Thank you, Mayor, for making our town a better looking place and just a better, safer place to live, with more effective law enforcement."

Some of our town employees have said, "Mayor, we will never forget what you did for us. We appreciate the pay scale improvements, our retirement and health insurance, our training, and everything else you gave us." Those are all wonderful accolades to receive from your associates.

But the one thing that pleased me more than anything else was the fact that I knew deep down that I had done my best in tackling a difficult job, with many opportunities for failure, and emerged with an ultimate victory. An assignment with failure stamped across each and every page is when the cream rises to the top and the satisfaction of accomplishment takes center stage. Generally speaking, if a job is not difficult, it's probably not worth doing. The job of mayor in Berry was worth doing, and I am grateful for the positive results produced from my 20 years in the role of mayor of my home town.

I am proud to have provided a service to my home town and to the home town of my parents and grandparents. I like to think that they would be proud of my efforts.

Friends Blessed the Pathway

I have been blessed through friendships I have made over the years. Growing up in a small rural town where most folks don't come to visit and very few drive through going elsewhere, friends were family, school buddies, and a small group in and around our town. I've already talked about my oldest and closest friends, Jimmy Barnes, T.A. Simpson and J.C. Shepherd. I am proud to say that they have been my bosom buddies for 75 years.

My early female friends were Barnell Dunn, Ruby Gay, and a few other elementary school girl friends in Berry. Barnell was special—a sweet blonde-haired cutie. I took a fancy to her in the second grade. It's funny how we remember little things, but I should say important little things. It was customary to exchange Valentine's cards in our second grade class at Berry Elementary, and I still recall the words printed on that little Valentine's Day card from my sweetheart Barnell. The card said, "Wouldn't it be rosy if we could get cozy."

My infatuation did not end there. I moved away from Berry in 1942 and again in 1946, however I never forgot Barnell. After I moved to Birmingham, I had an opportunity to visit with Barnell several times back in Berry. She later married Vernon Dorrough and had a lovely family. Upon my return to Berry in 1989 I had a chance to visit with Barnell in the final days of her life. She seemed pleased to revive our friendship. She pulled out an album of old pictures, and when she opened the front cover the very first picture was of her and me together. We reminisced about the days gone by, and I regret that we had only that one visit before she passed away. But I still remember her smiling face and the joy that my visit seemed to have brought to her eyes. We had many pleasant memories and were able to happily recall the days of our youth. It reminded me just how precious friendships in life really are.

One of our first visitors a short time after Phyllis, my mother, and I began our task of reclaiming Pleasant Hill Farm was another old friend. Phyllis and I were sitting on the back porch of our mobile home, which served as temporary housing while our house was being built, one afternoon when a stranger sporting a big cowboy hat waddled around the corner. I knew immediately that he had to be a friend from the past, but I wasn't quite sure who he was.

The stranger said, "You don't know who I am." I had to put my mind in another gear and go back to about 1943, but before he could get his name out, I declared, "You are T.A.

Simpson." A big, familiar grin came over his face as he said, "That's right." I told him that his walk and talk gave him away, and we sat for a spell and rehashed the good old days in Berry.

Jimmy Barnes and J.C. Shepherd also welcomed us home to Berry, and all of the names I have discussed provided us with a new sense of belonging. I was home among old friends, and it felt good.

I also made a new friend upon my return to Berry in Victor Thompson. Victor, also known as Captain Vic, was a former fishing boat captain in Key West, Florida, before he and his wife Sharon moved to Berry. Vic was the type of friend who dropped whatever he was doing to assist me in whatever needs that I had. I often remember times when we were out of water for days or even weeks. Vic and Sharon had well water, and they were generous. We would go to their house and bathe, then load up our water jugs with drinking water. It was better and probably much safer to drink than the Berry water was at that time. Vic and Sharon would return to the Keys to fish, and on their return we would be their guests for a super seafood bash. That kind of friendship is rare. Vic's friendship taught me a lot. Sometimes it is good to think of the needs of others before your own, and he was that kind of friend. We lost him all too soon. He died at a very young age, but we still have his memory and it will endure forever.

We make new friends in the strangest places. Phyllis and I were attending a business meeting in Savannah, Georgia, in 2008. We decided to take a break and enjoy a guided tour of beautiful Savanna.

We were sitting in the trolley station, waiting for our tour to begin. We observed a couple, apparently waiting for the same tour, then introduced ourselves, as did they. They were Wayne and Carolyn Brady, of Mobile, Alabama. They were avid fans of The University of Alabama fans just as we were for Auburn. The conversation opened the door for me to talk about my desire to write a book. What a coincidence, they were writers and shared my enthusiasm for publishing a novel. The friendship blossomed. I owe a great deal to both Wayne and Carolyn for all their help and encouragement, not to mention writing and rewriting segments of this book.

I made another new friend and rekindled some memories of Berry. This friend grew up after I left Berry. I met Delbert Reed and his lovely wife, Peggie, at McFarland Mall in Tuscaloosa when my son David and I were singing there one Sunday during a benefit for the West Alabama Muscular Dystrophy. I approached Delbert seeking help with locating our sound equipment, and we quickly got into a conversation and shared our memories of Berry and our love for our home town. I followed

Delbert's progress through his literary writings in the *Northport Gazette*, which included a story or two about Berry and the progress the town was making while I served as mayor. We became closer while Delbert was associated with the Paul W. Bryant Museum at The University of Alabama.

Phyllis and I met with Delbert several months ago and shared my desire to compose a book of my life experiences. Delbert read some of my feeble attempts to write and said he thought the material and subject matter had merit but agreed that I was in need of some help. Delbert had just finished his fourth book, so I was confident that he could help me with my book if he had the time. He graciously agreed to do just that. Delbert and I share many common thoughts and ideals. He has the innate ability to effectively put words on paper to illustrate and support a point of interest, and I am not certain that this book would ever have been published without his invaluable assistance. Phyllis and I are proud to have Delbert and Peggie on our list of friends.

My life has been greatly enriched through the many lasting friendships I have acquired. Bob and Marie Boone entered my life almost 40 years ago. They were there when Phyllis and I got married, and they have remained our friends since. They have always been there for us, and I appreciate them very much. We enjoy being together, and we visit with them frequently in Montgomery and they visit us in Berry. Phyllis and I married in Montgomery in 1973 and from that day to this we have been close friends.

Two others who are very dear friends are Jim and Evelyn Durough. I consider Jim and Evelyn VCFs (very close friends). They have been a part of our lives since the 1980s. Phyllis and Evelyn worked together at BellSouth in Birmingham. Jim and I became good friends as a result of our wives' association. Jim and Evelyn never fail to go out of their way to help friends. They are the epitome of friends.

As we march through this life we meet a lot of people. We meet and get to know a great number of folks, and one is truly blessed if he or she has a handful of close friends. My definition of close friends or DPF (dear and personal friends) means they are in this rare category. The people we have mentioned above all fall in that DPF category.

Ray Nelson, a dear friend and the mayor of Fayette, once asked me what I considered the crowning achievement of my 20 years as mayor of Berry. Before I could answer, he said, "I bet it was the improvement in the quality of drinking water." I agreed that solving Berry's water problems was probably our greatest accomplishment, but there were others of which I am proud.

I thank God for my friends. I recall the old Baptist hymnal, "What a Friend We Have in Jesus" and I am blessed to have Jesus on my side. I thank God for my friends; they have enriched my life and have been a stabilizing factor in my development. My association with each one has truly blessed my life. Thank you, my friends.

Final Thoughts

I have said a lot in this review of my life experiences, hoping to demonstrate that each one of us has many valuable life experiences. And, as you have seen, not all of them are good. I've also attempted to show that we can benefit even from those bad experiences if we evaluate the situation carefully and learn from it.

I urge you to always focus on life's big picture and not dwell on yesterday's problems. As my mother always said, "If you're looking back, you won't see what lies ahead and you might trip over it. Keep your eyes on your goals."

Try to get into the habit of seeing life as a whole. Widen your viewpoint. Each day is but a single step on a long journey. View each day as an opportunity for a new adventure and enjoy that day as one of life's wondrous gifts.

At the same time, try to widen your view of life. As a photographer, I know that a wide-angle lens will capture a bigger view of a scene that a normal lens. The same is true in life. You simply have to look at life with a wide-angle attitude.

You can make true, wonderful, meaningful, life-long friendships. You can achieve great things. You can inspire and help others by giving of yourself. And you can find success and happiness in doing all these things.

As I've said before, you simply have to put on your work boots and get busy doing whatever it is that you are called to do. And listen for that call. Opportunity knocks, but it doesn't always knock loudly. You have to be open to opportunities and willing to accept challenges.

No one will ask or expect you to do it all. You can be the captain or a part of the team. Either way, never be afraid to thrust yourself into the game of life. Work to improve yourself in every way every day and encourage others to do the same. One person can make a difference. One person can dream and lead and inspire many others. By doing more than you ever believed possible, probably the only person you surprise will be yourself.

Someone has said that you get out of life about what you put into it, and I believe that is true. I urge you to give a little more each day. I am certain that you will enjoy the results.

There is much joy to be found in life. I wish you success in finding that joy with those you love.

Acknowledgments

This was my first attempt to write a book. I certainly realized I could use some help. I knew I should seek assistance, and that is exactly what I did.

The following people contributed significantly:

Phyllis, my loving wife and constant supporter.

Wayne and Carolyn Brady, who assisted with data gathering, structure suggestions, and encouragement.

My daughter, Virginia Franklin, who constantly encouraged me to finish my book.

Joe and Joyce Dobbs, who provided family material and encouragement.

Joyce Jones, who edited and suggested ideas to strengthen particular sections.

Jim and Evelyn Durough, who reviewed drafts and edited for structure and grammar.

Michael Hammack, who provided computer technical support. I would have been drifting without his valuable assistance.

Delbert Reed, a multi-published author, who gave freely of his time and expertise.

Kaci Lane Hindman, who helped with the final edit.

These people, along with many others, provided encouragement and direction. I will be ever grateful and indebted to them.

Made in the USA
Lexington, KY
12 February 2019